Dream Catcher 31

July 2015

*To Sheena — irreplaceable
friend. Many thanks for
always being there.*

Love & best wishes,

Marion

X.

Stairwell Books //

Dream Catcher 31

SUBSCRIPTIONS TO
DREAM CATCHER
MAGAZINE

£15.00 UK (Two issues inc. p&p)
£22.00 Europe
£25.00 USA and Canada

Cheques should be made
payable to **Dream Catcher**
and sent to:

Dream Catcher Subscriptions
161 Lowther Street
York, YO31 7LZ
UK

+44 1904 733767

argillott@gmail.com

www.dreamcatchermagazine.co.uk
@literaryartsmag
www.stairwellbooks.co.uk
@stairwellbooks

Dream Catcher Magazine

Dream Catcher No. 31

ISSN: 1466-9455

Published by Stairwell Books //

ISBN: 978-1-939269-32-4

Contents – Authors

EDITORIAL

One of the joys of poetry, of fiction, is how they can both turn the world upside down, or create new worlds, as well as casting a sideways glance at the world we have. The wilder shores of science fiction and fantasy create self-contained structures where all the rules are different, the reader's imagination is stretched to understand a culture more alien than any on this planet, while nearer home writers tread along the borderlands between the real and the imaginary, the plausible and the seemingly impossible, between the living and the dead.

Dream Catcher 31 is particularly rich in work that takes across that line from where we are, comfortable, to another place, sometimes one which feels not at all familiar. We have Andrea Bowd's *The Loud and the Dead,* Philippa East's chilling inversion of the TV game show in *The 2000 Calorie Man,* Emily Drew's excursion into the world of zombie memory, and, less edgily, Sam Kemp's conversion of the writer's stock in trade, words, to currency.

It is a pleasure, too, to present sequences or groups of poems which reflect an author's continuous engagement with a subject. In this issue there is Marion Ashton in New Orleans, David Cooke in North East Lincolnshire, and Ann Heath in not Barmouth. In each case a real location is used to step off into other places of the mind.

The photographs by Ros Garland were so compelling that we decided to make an exception to our policy on photographs and invite her to be our featured artist. The 1970s and '80s are from a world that has largely disappeared and these photographs are a poignant reminder of what has been lost.

Looking forward to Dream Catcher 32, due out at the end of 2015, we are pleased to welcome Pat Borthwick, a well-known award winning poet, long associated with the Yorkshire Open Poetry Competition, as guest editor. As well as having a keen eye for the well constructed poem Pat is particularly interested in flash fiction and would love to see your submissions. Send to the usual address (see previous pages). Deadline for receiving copy for the next issue is 15th September 2015.

John Gilham

FEATURED ARTISTS

ARTIST STATEMENT: ROSALIE (ROS) GARLAND

I was always good at drawing and I made pocket money from drawing portraits as a kid. I wanted to be an illustrator and probably could have made a living from it. I actually got invited to judge some local art society exhibitions, I must have been fairly well regarded as an artist.

Then one day someone my mother knew said there was an old gypsy living on the Woldgate in Bridlington who had an interesting face and commissioned me to draw a portrait of him. I was in my first year at art college, I had to go out and take some pictures for my photography primer course that week anyway, it was cold and I didn't 'really' want to sit for hours drawing outside. So I thought I'd go and take a photo of the man to draw from. Mr Smith wasn't that keen on posing for a portrait but he wanted a picture of his dog, so I photographed them both. (It turned out that he was a cousin of another gypsy family I knew from my childhood).

I took the film home to develop it myself. I had bought the wrong type, it was something called XP1 and they didn't have the right chemicals at college. It's a wonder the film survived. But my tutors were very impressed with the photographs and made quite a fuss. I can't remember if that lady ever got her drawing, but I specialised in Photography after that.

I worked as a freelance, in Yorkshire and Lancashire through the eighties and nineties, photographing rural life and some of the traditional industries that were on the verge of disappearing at that point. I didn't just photograph other peoples' lives. I photographed my family life obsessively; my children as they were growing, not only birthdays and special occasions, but at play, fighting, first day at school, a visit to the dentists, ballet class, riding motorcycles. Because I used 35mm film, bought in 30 metre rolls and processed it myself, it was fairly cheap. I had 'almost' the freedom that carrying a smartphone camera gives everyone these days.

I went on to get my Masters Degree in Photography from the University of Derby. I was an early adopter of digital media, including VR which is becoming popular again. I still make photographs and I teach at the University of Lincoln.

Clients include;

The Arts Council, North West Arts Charities, Hull City Council, The Guardian newspaper, United Airlines.

2

My long term photography project on Motorcycle Culture is still a work in progress.

At the Mermaid Hotel in Rye

It's a seafaring room, its floor
    remembers the waves. The bed
        is chocked level, but chests of drawers
heel over as if close-hauled
    with sheets belayed.
        The mirror's silvering shows
where salt has splashed it and crowsfeet
    round the fittings have surely come
        from measuring weather
through long years. We stow
    our landsmen's clothes,
        bracing the wardrobe door
against the air. Its hinges tick.
    Two full miles from tides
        that swept up Dungeness
to hide behind, we are landlocked
    in a sea of grass. Windows look
        on yachts in what is left of the river,
their masts at mudbank angles. This room
    is drained of time.
        The mirror pockmarks our faces.

Barbara Cumbers

DINOSAUR FOOTPRINTS, ISLE OF WIGHT

The tide's retreated to the edge of sight,
a blur of birds and waves. I brush dried mud
of Chilton Chine down from my clothes,
fine dust scattering. *You should have held on to me*,
you say, as I might have done five years ago.

Dinosaurs had walked here once – huge feet
left prints on ripples in a delta's swamp,
and ripples turned to rock, and rock to shore.
Silt slides over older silt, continents buckle.
Iguanodon is twice transformed,

from beast to footprints, teeth and bones;
from Hawkins' horn-nosed quadruped
through lumbering biped to bird-like grace.
First built with little data, modified with more,
the past is always changing. You smile,

as you did five years ago when we'd collected
sediment for your research. And now
we work together at a fresh cliff face
revealed by winter storms and landslip,
uncovering more data cautiously.

Barbara Cumbers

*The model of an iguanodon in Crystal Palace Park was sculpted by
Benjamin Waterhouse Hawkins in 1852. Based on what had been
discovered at the time, it is now known to be wildly inaccurate.*

A TOURIST TOWN ON THE COAST

A terrible thing to be a tourist town,
settled in the bluff, angled on the off,
the ageing coast of a crumbling country,
a timid frown of coastline mapped each day.

An old town, a station, a terminus.
A cold Victorian seaside resort.

Little lanes join to form long streets,
follow the form of forgotten minds.
A resurrection of Tennyson's long line
amongst the muck and dirtrow.

Seaside architecture has its own school,
fluted ledges de rigueur these days,
panelled pastry edged in gilt-racked frost,
sullen in the modern glare, salted,
crusted, cracking for vanilla air.

Balconies scar the seafront like a riddle,
a stick of rock riven through,
a message of allegiance cried into lengths
of candy-coloured conformity,
ersatz lingua franca,
erstwhile empire of artefacts.

Tourists still tame the sea. But
also they are architects and poetry
students. They seek a long-stepped
time of stulted skirts, harnessed
to a cup-winner long since out to stud.

Jason Monios

I

Barmouth is Brill!
I did not get ill
On the fair,
Because it was shut.

II

We race along the edge of Wales,
slip between a slide of hills,
a flat of mud, a wild of water
stretched improbably to Aber,
churning high tide skies brown
and slow. We round a headland,
grind along a bridge, across
a foaming estuary, feel
the wind's hit, then
stutter into shelter in the guttering
of Cardigan Bay.

I have never been here before,
and yet I'm sure
I know it.

They have begun to batten down,
to spiral into winter.
The kiosks and the sweet shops
have shutters poised to lock
against the onslaught,
while buckets full of windmills rattle
rainbows into the sea breeze.
The fair is shut. The horses leer
insane from half-blown tarpaulins,
whales and lobsters gaze
across the puddled green of Crazy Golf.

This is eye-watering, leg-whipping weather.
This is the million tiny scratches from a towelling off,
stick thin children learning that teeth chatter,
before they burn their frozen fingers on their chips.
It is curtain-print dresses, trousers vacuum-packing shins,

the smell of sea foam and hairspray,
and all under the grand parental stare
of manses become B&Bs,
gables like grey bunting,
highest windows looking over
and out to sea.

This is the familiarity
of family holidays,
my cod nostalgia
for something
small and dull and wet.

Barmouth is the 70s again.
It is the end of season,
and I am learning to be uncomfortable.

III

She is all fury.
Crow hair, eyes set black,
berry-painted lips tight
in a pout that proves
she could sulk for England,
and probably does. She slams into her place,
claims the whole damn table –
rucksack, mobile, coke –
sticks her cartoon high-stacked
boots across the seat
and frowns at everything,
and nothing.

She cannot be twelve yet.
The world bores her.

The train pulls out, her
classmates scatter ice-cream pink
around her, giggle, chatter,
while in tidy notebooks,
they start to write close-packed
letters round as sweets,
poems called Our Holiday. She

8

takes her mobile, texts
her coruscating truth to someone else,
thumb nail flashing midnight blue
like ink.

"Poetry, dear," a teacher persists
in her ear, "Just try to say
what you will take away
with you. Your piece of truth."

She snorts disgust, rolls her eyes,
and then pulls out
a ratty notebook, thumbs to a page
already thick with doodles, and
Our Holiday in stark black lettering,
sharp as lightning, dripping globs
of coloured-in blood.

This I will want to read.
No cod nostalgia, no learning to be nice.
She will have hated it,
and she will say so with
the venom of the magnificently bored,
the spite of being young,
when everything is someone else's fault,
and you are helpless, blameless, caught,
with nothing else to do
but learn to swear, and sulk.

I crane to read these virulent insights.
"Barmouth is Brill!" she writes.

Ann Heath

WHEN YOU
WERE SEVEN

the kitchen glowed amber
in the glass

as you slipped through
the soft blue garden,

like a blackbird
chuckling into dusk.

Air, damp and calm
as mushroom,

stroked your skin,
your skirt grew heavy,

and in the lane,
orange sun, sinking,

dazzled your lashes,
lifted shadows through your hair.

Your name cried out
behind you,

like a seabird
for the sea,

and you thought "If
I don't go now,

when?"

Ann Heath

HOMEWARD

The slow haul back you think of little else
but a stamping ground less bleak than Faroes,
Fair Isle, Viking, but still have work to do.
Scouring, swabbing and sluicing down
the gangways, decks and quarters,
you grease moving parts, while all things
that shift and roll are stowed away,
until there's nothing out of place
to snag the agent's curmudgeonly gaze,
or give him scope to knock back your wages…

With a lathering of cheap carbolic soap,
some aftershave and a slap of Brylcreem
you'll scrub up yourself, good enough at least,
with cash on hip and a clean shirt,
for the tarts that shoal in shadows
around Riby Square or come across for trade
in the warm lee of certain boozers –
The Kent Arms, The Humber, the fractious
dives where ale flows freely
and mind-numbing gregariousness
absorbs the wad you've slaved for;
and while you're flush you'll pull her in,
some girl that's caught your eye –
her hands softer than braiders' hands,
but in their way as skilful.

David Cooke

IN THE HOLD

The first time you went below
you couldn't hear or think
of a thing: not even

your fear of slicing
a finger which in the cold
you might not notice.

And having lost
their rag with words,
reduced in all the din

to senseless
mouthings, the older men
spat curses, damning

youth's cack-handedness;
a rooky's lack of speed,
then showed you

once again
how to slit a belly
and scrape out its slops

with a tidy
off hand flourish.
Given time you'd

get the knack
as others had
before you –

the cloudless eyes
staring back
from layered beds of ice.

David Cooke

APPRENTICES
GRIMSBY C.1880

Consigned to the hellbound lurching
of smacks, we were a back street surplus,
a poorhouse dross with tainted blood.
Worth less than slaves or cattle
that have to be bought or reared,
we were the spillage of couplings
in damp infested rooms.

A lost brood of liars and thieves,
predisposed to mischief, we were damned
from the moment our lungs cleared –
swaddled in filth and howling.
Hollow chested, intractable, we were unfit
for a uniform or even a grave
on some frittering ledge of the empire.

So fetched up here instead
in this port of outlaws, signed over
to masters whose pockets jangled coin,
but soon grew intolerant
of stubborn mumblings
and fumbled attempts at fourteen
to match the skills and muscles of men.

For each God-bothering skipper
there were plenty more who'd bait us
or look the other way when deckies,
cooks and mates tried to tame us
with 'good natured ribbing'
that always went too far: their mock
'executions' and acts that 'never happened'.

We came in our thousands to learn
the value of a rudimentary trade,
with droves absconding to the haven
we found in Lincoln Gaol: written off,
released. Others perished hauling lines,
or slipped from the rigging, barely missed,
their details logged in a spindling script.

David Cooke

BRAIDER

Each day she views the world
through a puzzle of knots
and meshes. Inured to work

and harsh fibre,
she has toughened her hands
in meths and urine –

for softer hands
would blister and burn,
lacking the strength

her skill imparts
to labyrinthine cordage.
Cast on the water,

it's delicate
and seems a thing
composed of air –

sinking only
because it's weighted.
Hauled in, it tenses

against itself
and the flexing
load it gathers.

When the seas
have emptied
she will make a net

that serves no purpose.
As ornamental
as a tapestry,

it will speak
of the days she's spent
stooped and aching.

David Cooke

14

THE WIND

Wind
Wrap your arms around me
Dance whilst I breathe,
Tousle my hair.
At the summit I wait for your caress
Soft and warm like a lover in summer's heat,
Angry like a spurned wife through winter's storms.
You follow me to distant lands,
So as I lie somnolent on a foreign beach
You blow sand into the pages of my book
Your fingers reaching out,
Touching but never waiting to be held.
I have my words for you wind:
Breeze, squall, gust, gale
You puff of air, you draft, you waft,
The cunning zephyr of my laments,
A chatterer of leaves to counter my laughter.
You are the motion of air,
An anticyclone wrapped round low pressure,
Which I'll always need to breathe.

Clint Wastling

LISTENING

The river runs in the dark.
Unseen.
Just the sound I call "river".

Is there such thing as a river?

Approach the current at dawn's light.

Banks
Water rushing and bubbling
Rubbing against rocks and trees' roots

I want the river.
Its sound.
Its magic.

I will take it home:
Will be my river.

With cuddled gentle hands
Collect the passing water into a bowl.

The liquid stills.
Only shakes with the trembling of my hands.

"My river, river of mine"
I cry silently,
"stay with me"

The water quietens.

Unhappy or playful? The water
 stares at me with glazed eyes.

With my fingers
I write my name
On the surface.

Kneeling slowly by the bank,
I extend my hands
and return its contents to the current.

Free
The water joins the flow

And bubbles down.

River once again?

For a time
I seem to hear it laughing
Joining the current,
Or is it cries of pain
As it hits the rocks?
Or is it whistling
Spiralling in dancing whirlpools
Rolling along the bank?

My name no longer in it.

The water I called "my river" is gone.

The river rushes..

Am I still here?

Differently now!

João Sousa

"Felicitations mes braves. Of all the Emperor's soldiers, you two are tonight the furthest into Portuguese territory. Not even the Imperial Guard can claim this accolade. This donkey-bridge over a piss-flow stream is at the forefront of French military honour. Guard it well. I shall be in the hovel, sleeping, and I do not want to be disturbed unless we are attacked. The colonel is in the village and he wants to be disturbed even less than I. If you live, live quietly. If you die, try to make a noise when you do it. Your muskets are for sounding the alarm. If you see the enemy, fire at once. Do not waste time trying to aim. And if you fire because you have pissed your pants at the sight of a shadow in the dark, I will have the skin off your back. Bonne nuit."

"Fat pig. How is it that the army is starving but the sergeants are still fat?"

"That is how they become sergeants. They stand you on parade and the first man to produce a capon and a bottle of wine is given the job."

"Look at him, waddling back to his pile of straw like the fattest boar on the farm. His lantern swings like a ship at sea, such is the way he has to move his legs around his great belly."

"You are jealous because he has a bed and a roof over his head."

"Surely. Who would not be? How shall we guard this bridge?"

"How shall we guard it? What are you – a general who must decide on the deployment of his forces? There are only two of us and but one bridge."

"Even so, what shall we do? Shall we both stay on one side or stand one here and the other over the stream? Or shall we walk back and forth across the bridge?"

"You do what you like. I will walk as I watch. It is the only way to keep my toes flesh instead of ice."

*****

"Jacques, Jacques. Come and look at this. There is a monkey here."

"A fine friend you are."

"What? What are you talking about?"

"It is three hours that we are here and not a drop of brandy has passed my lips but you have drunk so much that you are seeing monkeys."

"Brandy? I have no brandy. There is a monkey here. I did not know that there were monkeys in Portugal."

"There are not. For monkeys you must go to Africa or The Indies. In Portugal there is only bare ground, hard men and harder women. Let me see. Where is this monkey?"

"There. Sitting on that boulder. Do you see? Now, tell me, what is that if not a monkey?"

"You are right. It is a monkey. How has it come here?"

"How should I know? Do you think that I have had time to start a conversation with it?"

"Perhaps it is from a gypsy. Gypsies have monkeys."

"Gypsies? Do you see any gypsies around here? We are in the mountains with nothing but sheep and soldiers for miles around. Who do you think is going to need their fortune telling out here?"

"Gypsies are everywhere. Besides, there is the monkey in front of you, how else do you think it got here?"

"Perhaps it ran away...from a ship. Ships have monkeys."

"A ship? How much of that brandy have you drunk? Do you think that this ship ran aground two hundred miles from the sea?"

"I said that the monkey ran away. The ship could still be in harbour and the monkey here."

"It must be a bad ship indeed for the monkey to run two hundred miles away."

"What shall we do with the monkey? Shall we catch it?"

"Why? Do you think it is a spy?"

"No, but we could keep it on a piece of string. People like monkeys – they think they are adorable. With that monkey we could attract some of the women in the village."

"I've seen the women in the village – I'd rather kiss the monkey."

"Come on. Let's catch it. You distract it while I get behind it and put my hat over it."

"Distract it? What makes you think that I know how to distract a monkey?"

"Just make some noises."

"Hey monkey...little monkey...chuck, chuck, chuck."

"What are you doing? It's a monkey, not a chicken."

"I don't know what noises a monkey makes."

"Never mind. It doesn't seem scared. It's just sitting there like it wants us to catch it. Now, come on, nice and slowly. Here monkey, how would you like a nice piece of garlic sausage, eh?"

A soft fluttering and the rapid shuffle of light steps from behind, then the feel of cold, sharp steel on two throats.

"Buo noite, meus amigos. You are wasting your time with that sausage. Captain Macaco is a vegetarian."

Kevan Youde

Gypsy Dog
Woldgate, Bridlington, 1981

THIS TIME LAST YEAR

At first we didn't hear the Fates
Singing over the ice locked land,
Saw only hoar frost,
Breathed in fog.
In our mouths the taste of snow.

When the owls carried his name
Through the darkness around the house
We allowed through the cracks
Only owl talk
Un-translated,
While, out on the hill,
The ewe lamb broke into the pheasant bin,
Filled her belly with corn
And died.

Is a man's life no less precarious than that?

He phoned us,
This time last year.
Familiar voice warm and lively
But bringing with it
A strange unfamiliarity -
The sound of the Fates
Who already knew
What he and we did not.

Julie Baber

CHALKING UP
ANOTHER

With a tinsey
Tipping down
Of my chin
I see
Another birthday
Slightly wheezy
On a silvering
Horizon
More keys
To the bunch
To be dropped
By an absent
Mind
Another trip
To the loo
My darling
Added
To the others
Trod
Through the hours
Of slumber
And days
Ticked off
Before yesterday
Is even dry

Vennie

KAFKAESQUE   Kafkaesque?
              Kafkaesque?
              Sod it, chum, it ain't the best!

              Minding his own business,
              taking care of this and that,
              beavering away in his own little flat.
              Then it's all "Mr K you done that,
              that thing, what we ain't gonna tell ya.
              But, trust me, you're as guilty as hell, yeh."

              And they're gone, and it's silence.
              No pressure, no violence.
              Mr K's left to stew in his juices,
              and dream after dream of hangmen and nooses.

              Kafkaesque?
              Kafkaesque?
              Leave it out, I do not jest!

              But what's this? Something through the door.
              Official letter menaces on the floor.
              Be there, this time, that day.
              Don't even think of running away.

              So he gets himself down there.
              He's living the nightmare.
              Still got no idea why
              he's in the frying pan, ready to fry.

              Kafkaesque?
              Kafkaesque?
              What a kerfuffle, what a mess!

              It's a long, long story
              and the ending is gory.
              Thankfully, at least it's quick and fatal
              unlike the slow decay of man-turned-beetle.

              But that's for another time.

              Or, perhaps not:
              (Blues riff) I woke up this mo'nin'
              I've turned into a beetle ... oh, shit!

              Steve Allen

24

ONE STEP BEYOND

I didn't know you until I was in my thirties
but by the end of the decade we were on

first name terms. I remember our first words
in a cold room at the chapel of rest;

I knew you were a bit bloody weird then,
beaming with pride at a job well done.

You even said: "It looks like him, dunt it?"
referring to my scrubbed up dad, on your slab.

It was Yorkshire empathy at its best.
I wanted to say you'd been inappropriate

but what could possibly be appropriate
in the presence of the dead?

Since then, you've done my mum, neighbours, an old school friend,
and each time I see you, the closer we become.

I've even dreamt about you in your black suit,
and a bowler hat, playing the trumpet for Madness

to *One Step Beyond*, like some cockney grim reaper.
But you've never ventured down the M1-

you've been far too busy
burying those I've lost and loved.

One day, you waved at me from your hearse –
I waved back. We were like bus drivers

who'd known each other for years.
Listen: don't take this the wrong way mate

but can you just pretend you don't know me?
No offence, but please, just look the other way.

Mark Connors

ONE STEP CLOSER

He appears across the road,
Hadrian, the local undertaker,
locking up after a busy day at work,
taking my measurements
from eyes on the back of his head;
I'm only suffering from runner's knee.
Perhaps he senses something that I don't;
he knows my family history all too well.
He can't resist a loaded wave. I wave back,
trying hard to look as healthy as I can.
I bumped into him in Morrisons last week.
"Hello, Mark," he said, in his deep dark drawl
as I opted for the low-fat crisps;
more reasons to do my shopping somewhere else.
Now, he marks the slow progress to my car.
His smile is wide but not quite right,
like those constructed daily for the dead
when he readies them for grievers.

Mark Connors

THE LOUD AND THE DEAD

Sometimes they listen to me,
when the wind has stopped wailing and there's no sound
of raindrops on gravestones. So I wait until calm has descended

over the churchyard. Then firmly but politely,
 I explain that shouting insults
when I'm travelling on buses is inappropriate and

proves embarrassing when
I loudly retort in a disturbed tone,
"You've GOT to stop it."

The dead whisper amongst themselves but agree,
promising that they will, in future,
be discreet.

Andrea Bowd

Smokes stood on the roof of his apartment building looking out over the destroyed city below. After lighting up a cigarette, he took a tattered wallet from his scruffy green jacket. He opened it and shook out a little chain of pictures, the kind you get in photo booths at theme parks. Among the string of pictures was a slightly younger, less bitter looking, non-infected version of himself with a lovely red-head woman. One picture showed them all cute and hugging, another of the girl showing off an engagement ring, another of a much younger brunette boy photo-bombing the couple, and the last an image of the non-infected Smokes pulling the other boy in and giving him a noogie.

The zombie sighed sadly and folded the pictures back. Not wanting to put the wallet away, he poked into the various openings, glancing at useless coins and paper money. Then he flipped through the collection of cards until he found his old driver's license. He took the card out for a better look, reminding himself of how hard it was for him to get it.

~*~

A sixteen year old Frank Anderson sat in the back seat of his father's car, with his best friend as they were driven to his first driver's test. "Ok man, you got this," Mark told Frank as they pulled into the DMV.

After a long wait inside, Frank was able to take the test. At first he was doing pretty well, just as he had been practicing. However several times he went over the speed limit, passed a stop sign, and took a turn a bit too hard going briefly into the other lane. Luckily there were no cars there at the time. He failed the test.

~**~

Three years later, for Frank's fourteenth go at the driving exam, Mark walked with him to the DMV. Once Frank started the testing car, it was all going pretty well, until he almost caused a road block by driving too far forward for a turn on a narrow street. Just that wouldn't have been too bad, but shortly after, he struggled to parallel park, and stated out loud how he should have practiced parking more.

~**~

When Frank was twenty-three he was on driving test number thirty and doubted he would ever pass. "You know, don't be too hard on yourself man, I mean, some people just aren't *meant* to drive." Frank shot Mark a sour glare as they headed once again to the DMV. "I mean, there's

28

always the bus, riding a bike and hey! Walkin's healthy!" Mark snickered when Frank flipped him off.

The test, just like all the others, started out well. As it went on, it continued to go smoothly. He didn't go over the speed limit, didn't go too fast on turns, stopped at stop signs and red lights, and even remembered to check the mirrors and buckle up before starting off. The Instructor also seemed pleased with how Frank was doing, and as the test neared its end, he told him all that was left was to reverse into a space once they were back at the DMV.

Frank nodded and, after signalling, turned into the parking lot. As carefully as he could he tried to back into a spot, however he felt just letting it roll in was going far too slowly, so he tried to give it a little gas.

He gave it a little too much gas and hit the car in the spot just behind the one he was trying to back into, which happened to be the instructor's car.

Frank gave an audible groan once the instructor got out of the car after crossing off the "pass" note on his clipboard.

Maintaining his push for the maximum four tests a year, Frank had reached driving test number forty-three by the time he was twenty-six. He dragged his feet while Mark once again pulled him along to the DMV. "C'mon, 43's the charm! Statistically speaking, you have to pass eventually!" Frank just sighed and went in to stand in line.

When the test started Frank tried to push down feelings of dread and just focus on doing everything right. Keeping it at the speed limit he carefully followed all the instructions and this time when backing in at the end he didn't give it any extra gas.

Much to Frank's amazed delight he was told he passed. He had failed forty-two times but finally passed on the forty-third try.

Smokes was brought back to the present by hearing his name. Mark, now a zombie too, was using his hands to stand on the roof ledge in front of him.

"You here now? You were just staring off into space for a while."

Smokes blinked before nodding and putting his driver's license away. "Yeah, yeah... just remembering something..."

Mark gave him a pat on the shoulder before hopping down from the ledge. "Well no time to dwell on the past. C'mon! I have something *big* planned!"

"What for?" Smokes asked after realizing the cigarette he had lit earlier had burnt out while he was remembering some of his driving exams. He started to light up another.

Mark grinned. He half hoped his pal would have forgotten, just so he could enjoy the reaction. "Remember? Your 40th birthday!" Smokes coughed, dropping his lighter and cigarette while Mark laughed. "C'mon, let's go be old zombies in style."

Emily Drew

IMPERCEPTION

Remembering,
I see myself looking,
not what I saw.

Sometimes distant:
a burnt-out classroom cycled past
from as far away again.

Sometimes askew:
I look over my shoulder
at you naked on summer grass.

Sometimes perceived:
it is your view I know
of my fall from a crag.

Sometimes –
no, not going there
from anywhere.

Memory becomes a third,
mediating between scene and eye;
we see only what we want.

As blurred days begin
will I look back wryly
to when I had a choice?

Grahaeme Barrasford Young

The night before my father died he opened his mouth to speak, stopped and breathed hard, as if struggling to free his last words from nets of resentments and regrets.

'If I had my time over again, I'd go all out for myself, *I wouldn't give a damn about anybody else.*'

It was 1976. That same year I had the chance to join a friend starting a charter airline, a sunrise industry in the '70s. I said no. I've never really understood the life of the entrepreneur. How can you just go out and buy a dozen planes before you've got a customer? What if no one rings you up to buy a seat? Not for me marking out my own stamping ground in some commercial wilderness on the economy's newest frontier. No. I wanted a road atlas and very clear directions for a risk-free route through life. I stayed where I was, in local government.

And now for almost forty years I have negotiated the borderland of the commuter journey, neither work nor leisure, every day of every working week, except for annual 'flu and last year's stress.

These walks to catch the bus were more than just the way to get to work. After only a few months they were a hobby; I collected precious dawns and fine sunsets, photos in a filing cabinet second-hand from work. Why not, if stamps and china, why not skies? Even now, from May to September, I work overtime so that when I'm walking home the western sky might burn vermilion and black flames fleck the hills of Wales.

Thirty years or so ago the walks became religious and now each time I leave the house a daily pilgrimage begins. A frosty sunrise, the eastern sky in goldfish scales, the air so clear and hard you could scratch your name upon it, is God's reward for vigils patiently endured through mornings of drizzle and evenings of sleet. And so it has been, year after year.

My father was wrong, in a way, his last words to me were wrong. In a sense, *I've* had his time over again and I've done exactly what he did: a job for life, a routine and glimpses of the eternal not fully understood.

Graham Dawson

BORDERLAND

Dusk lends itself to marsh
The last of the light
Drawn down into amber pools
And the luminous bodies of little egrets.
Land, by day unsure of its status,
Merges, as evening settles,
Into sky and water.
The hard line of the shingle bank its only definition.

Now this land,
Made through generations of hard toil,
Is given up in sacrifice to the sea,
Flocks evacuated to more stable ground
Harbour curlew
Whose mournful voice
Belies the joy of its returning.

Amidst the rustling of unseen beings
A stoat scuttles out beneath the nose of dog
Who pounces – too slow
While ghost birds
Come to roost in the skeletal remains
Of trees that drank salt and died;
A slow motion collapse
Into the graves of ancient ancestors
That grew here long ago.

This is borderland with no border.
Light, space, time
Ebb and flow
Defying all notion of conformity.
Solid objects shape-shift
Into unknown liquid entities
And wind whips whispering grasses into waves.
This is borderland.
Its ever changing nature
Its only permanence.

Julie Baber

BONE CHINA

Imagine if instead of seeping
into thirsty soil
the days of our lives

had pattern and form,
amounting to something
we could identify,

a single long poem perhaps
or a vessel we could wrap
our hands around

and hold up to the light,
a comfortable sphere
with a frieze of painted flowers brighter

than anything else in the room –
poppy, primrose,
grass-of-Parnassus –

interlaced
on a ground of flawless
glistening white.

Ruth Sharman

SKY

When the sun brushes the clouds from the sky
you feel its simmer painted on your skin.
The air stipples your nostrils with dryness.

On days like this the sky is smooth
like running fingers over endless glass;
no ridges, no fissures; worn away Braille.

When there's heaviness pounding in your ears,
atmosphere wet with damp leaves' peaty scent,
cordite thunder shifts wardrobes overhead.

On days like this the sky is lumpy;
crowded with immoveable boulders, fear
pushing like a crush of Christmas shoppers.

Standing on sand near sea lapping shingle;
sky is the breeze whipping your hair askew,
ebbing the gull-song into the distance.

On days like this the sky is vastness;
how far above you does air become sky?
You reach up and touch the substance of space.

Sue Spiers

THE BENT AND TWISTED

The bent and twisted star under which
Our love was born
Long ago wrapped up its life and died,
Its packeted discharge carried leaping
On its space-crazed journey for so many aeons,
No wonder it was slightly mad
When it arrived – it slapped
Our amazed innocent faces
Upturned, looking for
Just a little bit of harvest from the heavens
And a lift from our humdrum lives.

Our love was great but our star
Was bent and twisted.
We keep baby hunchbacks like that.
We keep old grannies like that,
Raku pots and oak trees, country lanes,
And complicated keys and chains,
Artistic walking sticks and such-like wrought artefacts,
But not the crooked love that cannot leap
Across the first stile or ditch it comes to,
        Slips on a measly sixpence,
    Skids on shit
– No, this we take and in our mercy, shoot.

Clive Donovan

Marshland

In the time it takes to say
    you could have drowned,
        the marsh pools have gone quiet
            and the only sound is the drip
                drip dripping of your coat and hair.

                What's dry is your expression,
            that stunned prequel to either
        laugh or cry, and in the time
      it takes me to say you could
have drowned, you choose laugh.

I told you to follow me
    to nudge the soil for waves
        and test how keen it is to fill
            your bag, boots and pockets
                and show you how black black can be.

                Now I shout, and you cry.
            With your present and future sucked
        into the earth, in a kind of
      pre-packaged burial,
I'd never find the remote.

Into the mud with you
    goes the broadband password
        our exact anniversary date
            the birthdays of our friends
                and hours of pillow-talk exposition.
            The recycling set-up
          and feel of your collar bones
      the right printer ink
    the balance of boiling and egg
the successful flirtation with ticket inspectors.

The feel of your collar bones.
Damp hair in bed.
See all that can be left drifting

      in   the   night

        in the time it takes to say

                don't

                    step

                        there.

Sam Kemp

By the campfire
Woldgate, Bridlington, 1981

Breast is best, but Dumples is better! Max sats for your baby!

Clarks' new SELF-TYING shoe-laces! You'll never have to bend again!

Thigh chaff spoiling your summer? Strollacrem heals as it soothes!

Melly and Babra were watching TV. The Wrap-a-Round cast a sheen over the walls and across the curtains, drawn against the sun. Babra flipped through the channels.

'Great British Eat Off's on at six,' she said. 'What'll we watch till then?'

She lay length-ways on the sofa, bolstered against the cushions. Her feet, in bulbous socks, dangled off the end.

'Whatever's on,' said Melly. 'Just don't keep fidgeting.'

Babra put down the remote. Melly engaged the foot-rest of her chair.

Swooping music bounced from the TV speakers.

'Welcome back! Welcome back!'

A man in a purple suit filled the screen. He had shiny skin and cheeks like stretched balloons.

'That's Promb Weeber,' said Babra. 'Isn't he gorge?'

'Mm-hmm,' said Melly. 'Who?'

'Game shows, Mum. Dead famous.'

Melly chomped on a biscuit. On screen, the studio audience clapped and cheered.

'Tonight's contestant,' purred the host, 'is here to raise awareness of – ahum-hum – a somewhat small issue.'

The audience tittered. Promb's jowls joggled; he was trying not to smile. The Wrap-a-Round screen dimmed as the cameras panned across the crowd: rows of faces like marshmallows under the lights. Words scrolled along beneath: ...CONSUMES JUST 2,000 CALORIES A DAY!...

Down the steps at the side of the stage came a man, in a white suit with horizontal stripes.

'Holy crap,' said Babra.

'Language,' said Melly. But she felt the shock too.

Promb waited while the audience contained themselves, then waved his guest into a chair: 'Great to have you on the show.'

'Look at the room in that seat,' said Melly. 'He barely takes up half.' She peered down at the wide expanse of her own thighs, in their green jogging bottoms.

'Ouch,' said Babra. 'His knuckles stick out.'

'Tell me,' said Promb, spreading out his arms. 'How long have you had this problem?'

'I guess,' said the contestant nervously, 'since primary school. The one rickety kid in the class? That was me.'

Melly plucked at the neck of her blouse. A memory slid into her thoughts and away again, like a fish rising through gloomy waters.

She pushed her hand into a fresh pack of crumpets.

'Just goes to show,' she said to her daughter. 'Start off on the rickety side and end up like that.'

'Alright, Mum,' said Babra, opening a bag of crisps. 'Don't bang on.'

The Wrap-a-Round scrolled on: ...BMIs BELOW 30 ON THE RISE...

There was a scratching sound at the living room door. In waddled a wide, squat dog, with a stomach that bumped the floor. Melly scooped up her pet and settled him onto her lap. She fed him a gingernut and had one herself. His tail thumped against her knees.

'– causes so many problems,' the man went on. 'Like... sorry. This is embarrassing.'

Promb's shoulders quivered with jolly kindness. He squashed his fingers together and rested them on the swell of his stomach. 'Go on,' he said. 'We're all friends here.'

'On aeroplanes, say. I need extra cushions to wedge me in.'

'Imagine if that was Dad,' said Babra, tipping the crisps out into a bowl.

'Don't be silly. Your dad wouldn't get like that.'

'Not on your meal-plans.'

'There we go then.' Melly took up a second plate of biscuits from the trolley at her side. 'He just needs to eat more.'

Babra frowned and stuffed a handful of cheese puffs into her mouth.

'...And people call me names,' the thin man was saying.

'Really?' The host lolled his head from side to side. 'What sort of names?'

'You know... "Tight-ass." "Misery-guts."'

'Dear dear,' said Promb, his chins swaying. 'Have a tissue.'

Memories rose again through the murk of Melly's thoughts: taunts in the playground. She pushed a tea-cake into her mouth and sank her hands into the dog's comforting folds.

'I'm fat now,' she reassured herself. 'Fat.'

'Look how he fidgets,' she said out loud. 'He should try sitting still.'

'He's probably just nervous.'

'That's hardly an excuse.'

...COLD SENSITIVITY, INCREASED BODY HAIR, REDUCED FAT-TO-MUSCLE RATIO...

'Are these crisps new?' said Babra. 'They taste different.'

'Hmm?' said Melly. 'Oh. Better for you. More saturates.'

'But I liked the other ones.'

'Well...' said Melly. 'Those clothes I bought you last month were getting a bit loose.'

Babra hitched down her size-20 t-shirt, tucking it under her so the material stretched tight.

A woman in the audience pressed her buzzer. The overhead mic came winging her way; a pudgy hand reached up to grasp it.

'But ain't that it?' she said, swelling up in her chair. 'You don' enjoy your food, you spend nowt in the supermarkets. I fink people get skinny coz they're borin' an' mean.'

Promb leaned back and spread his cushiony palms. 'Well now.'

'I can't help it,' said the contestant, fiddling with his shirt collar. 'I see all this food and know I should be eating, but it's like.... after two or three cakes, I just feel... full.'

A murmur rippled through the audience.

'"Full"? Full of what?' The host's face was wide and curious.

'Just... full up. Something in my head says "stop".'

'Oh-h-h... Something in your head?' Promb's eyes glinted. 'Then could it be –' he leaned forward conspiratorially '– psychiatric? Ahum-hum! Join us after the break!'

Swooping music played them off.

Fat-Fast! 200 calories in just one bite!

Sleepeazy! Our reinforced beds are worth the weight!

Padded Spanx! The ultimate fill-out wear!

'That woman in the audience,' Babra said as they watched the ads, 'was proper harsh. He can't help it.'

''Course he can,' said Melly, demolishing a Mars bar. 'Told you, he just needs to eat more.'

'Yeah, well, I know how he feels. Eating gets lame. I mean, it's like, all we do.'

'Don't talk rubbish.' Melly stroked the dog and recited: '"Eat, eat, eat till the day's complete!"'

Babra pushed her cheese puffs round her bowl.

'Now then,' said Promb, re-appearing on-screen. 'We've a very special prize in store for you this evening, if you can pass our challenge. But before that – kindly step up on these scales here.'

Numbers rippled onto the display board above the stage: 10st. 3lb. The audience covered their mouths and shook their heads.

'Honestly,' said Melly. 'What does he live on – carrot sticks?'

Promb gleamed. 'And now, let's welcome my beautiful assistants!'

'Like it's so bad,' said Babra. 'If everyone was rickety, it wouldn't even matter.'

'Don't be ridiculous,' said Melly. 'How could that happen?'

'We'd all just eat less.'

Melly tutted. 'Shush. I'm trying to watch.'

On screen, two buxom blondes rolled onto the stage, carrying between them a Krispy Kreme box. Meanwhile, Promb buckled the man into what looked like a dentist's chair.

'Our contestant here must eat all twenty – and no chewing-and-spitting!'

The blondes descended, giggling and pouting as they fished out the sticky pastries.

'Haven't you finished those crisps yet?' said Melly.

Babra's bottom lip stuck out. 'I'm bored of eating. And I hate lying around all day.'

Melly snorted. 'Like you've so much else to do.'

One-by-one the assistants pushed the donuts into thin man's mouth. His eyes watered and the veins on his neck stood out.

'So what if I don't eat sometimes. What do you care anyway?'

Melly frowned. 'That's enough, Babra.'

Babra's jaw tightened. 'Why can't you like me the way I am? I am trying, you know. It's not my fault I'm tall for my age.'

'Don't start.'

'You're always going on at me! Why can't you leave me alone?'

'One more bite!' cheered the TV audience. 'One more bite!' With Promb's help the thin man choked down a last sugar-stuffed mouthful. The crowd went wild.

'Because.'

'Because what?'

'Because –' a flush rose up through Melly's chest '– because no daughter of mine is going to be – thin!'

The final word was almost a shriek. The dog yelped. On the screen, Promb and his guest were shaking hands: 'Congratulations! We're sending you to America! Fat Camp. That'll help you.'

Babra looked down at the mound of crisps in her lap, glistening with oil.

Then, very slowly, she set the bowl aside.

'I'm sorry, Babra,' said Melly. 'That came out wrong.'

'Actually, Mum –'

'What?'

'You're totally right.'

Melly hugged the trembling pet. 'I am?'

'Oh sure. I mean, you're only trying to help.'

'Well of course, Babra.'

'You heard what all those people said. You couldn't have me ending up like that guy. Like some weirdo. Some freak.'

Melly's eyes darted back and forth from the TV to her daughter. 'Well, people can be cruel.' She swallowed. 'So there'll be no more silliness?'

'No more silliness,' Babra echoed. She levered herself onto an elbow. 'In fact, I'm suddenly very hungry.'

'Really?'

'Oh yes. I feel like I could eat a horse.' Babra swung her legs round and down, and pushed herself into a sitting position.

'Where are you off to? Dinner's not for half an hour.'

'Like I said, I've got a real craving.' Her eyes were fixed on the goodies in Melly's lap.

'Oh.' Melly looked about her. 'Well, what would you like? Some biscuits? A jam tart?'

Babra stood.

'No-o,' she said. 'Something savoury.'

'Sausages-on-sticks? A pork pie?' Melly flailed a little in her chair, her plump hands scrabbling at the packets.

'Not quite.'

'Look, Babra, please sit down – think how many calories you're burning!'

'Don't worry.' Babra took a step forwards 'I know what'll put a few pounds back on.'

She leaned down. She stretched out her hands. Melly gasped as the warm bundle was yanked from her lap. There was a snap, a crunch, and a strangled bark.

Babra held a hairy drumstick in her fist.

The lifeless dog dropped into the crisp bowl. Babra sank back onto the sofa and gnawed away, glassy-eyed. On screen, the 2,000 calorie man was replaced by the Great British Eat Off. Credits rolled and the swooping music smoothed and soothed. Babra turned to Melly, sitting shell-shocked in her chair. A small red dribble ran down her chin as she spoke:

'Now that's enough screaming, Mum. Eat up.'

Philippa East

CARDINAL

There were Cardinal days when *unwelcome*
shone in bright red on the doorstep,
glowing with scope for the sin of dirtiness.
Ready to stain and be stained
it smelt of spirit, like mothered grazes,
so I wonder now the taste
that kissing better must have had.

Don't put your dirty feet there.
Take your dirty hands off that.
There was always something
that could be cleaner, that needed wiping,
mending, tying back,
something that was my fault.

She is still there in my garden
guiding secateurs and shears in weekly chores,
frowning at uncut edges, at clippings left lying.
I imagine her polishing the patio to Cardinal redness.

It's strange that my house is so free of her,
that clothes are not folded neatly, or hung
from well-spaced hangers, that knickers
are not ironed, that papers pile up.
There is dull brown paint on the front step.
It lasts for years.

Barbara Cumbers

STEAMED PLUMBING

Most winter days, hot water came in spurts
from every tap, even those marked 'C'.
The only one not hot was drinking water
in the butler sink low in the scullery.

And once in a while every tap was icy,
the day the range was raked, re-laid, re-lit;
the day the kitchen filled with ash
then logs, then coal, then smoke; the range

that squatted glowering in its niche.
My mother spent the morning on her knees
feeding it, then feeding it some more,
coaxing the burning of her offering.

I knew it wasn't God, but still
there were commandments set in iron
– thou shalt honour thy boiler when alight;
thou shalt not let the scuttle become empty.

It smelt of heat and long-dead cooking,
sent vulgar bubbling noises through the house
by secret pipes that seethed in boxed-in corners.
Outside, the overflows steamed gently.

Barbara Cumbers

Some penitents feared voice recognition, queued
in other churches. Most were like sprinters,
in and out of the confessional box
before you could finish a Hail Mary.

Youngsters like me eavesdropped, failed to comprehend;
'And did you come, my child?' 'And did you do in return?'

There was comfort in this communal act of revelation,
being cleansed weekly from the grime of sin.
I walked light-headed from confession determined
not to steal my neighbour's pen or covet his bike.

The panels of these booths were sooted with sin.
Confession was the Marmite, the honey,
which gelled church and church-goer.
There were no rulers to beat you with,
no missing your playtime, or writing one hundred lines.

Sins decomposed as you rose from your knees
and you felt you could get ten out of ten
for spelling and just might be chosen
for the school team, as a reserve.

Owen Gallagher

CROC-GOD

The crocodile doesn't see you as you,
you as you are from your point of view,
the life you have lived, your quality-smile.
If God in the sky is a crocodile,
don't expect mercy; he'll be a machine -
all muscular jaws with teeth in between
and a corkscrew motion for dragging you down
and holding you under water to drown.

Nor will it matter what you have done,
whether you worshipped him or the sun,
who you had sex with, the prayers that you said,
or others say for you now you are dead.
Nothing will cut much ice on the day;
he'll tear you apart, whatever you say,
and gulp you down with no more to do
than he would another who wasn't a you.

Richard Livermore

FRIEND OF THE EARTH

People sometimes make me feel
Like a lowly thing, a worm –
Do you love worms ?
They coil under flagstones
Glistening and fat, they warmly wriggle
I'd love to have one nestle on my empty palm
Right now, like a companion.
They're not holier than thou, nor the
Doubleted grandees of the world.
They're children not horrid adults who sneer.

A worm is soft and squishy
Not a hard case
Worms are brown and beautiful
Sneaking through long grass
Animals may like to eat them
But I've always treated them with care
They make such lovely, aesthetic worm hills
And live underground without a sound
Silky and silent they slither around.

So if you too think you resemble this
Humble creature, this makes me
Happy and snug feeling true to Mother Nature

And how lovely, finally, to be nibbled by them
As if with tender, beery kisses
Loved all over !

Angela Morkos

CARE – CAN BITE

We reach a stalemate;
you, a rigid ball of fury on the table
me, white knuckled on the muzzle straps,
even the intention of movement
a trigger to the circuit we've made.

We consider our options;
I need to poke and tease out the clues,
you want to curl around your hurt,
pinch and nip it away with none
of my intrusion on your fierce pride.

You decide - flick the switch
and in the hot breath of a quarter
second I feel the caution of teeth
and am left with the muzzle and a space
between us I can only admire.

Ilse Pedler

Derick Bannantyne had spent his life waiting for a hippo. The fact that there used to be a hippo at Chester Zoo is not surprising in itself but that Bannantyne waited for it is. It makes perfect sense if I tell you that Derrick Bannantyne was a taxidermist, a frustrated one, but a taxidermist by profession all the same.

Bannantyne had been employed by the Liverpool Civic Museum twenty years before I went to work there. He spent his years sitting in an airless, subterranean office surrounded by large freezers and several long-dead animals, all of which he was re-stuffing while the public could watch him work through a small window. Socially the museum was fairly restricted. Bannantyne would meet people in the lift and engage in light-hearted banter and, on occasion, join the Egyptologists for coffee and cakes. Of all his colleagues he was drawn to them the most, undoubtedly because they, like him, had an interest in the moribund. In addition to Egyptologists, Bannantyne liked young women and all of us were at some point subjected to his slightly unsettling remarks which were invariably in bad taste. We felt sorry for Bannantyne, he had little to recommend him and as he was always accompanied by a clewing odour of chemical preservatives – few sought him out. Other than that I know very little about him and less about the elderly hippo in Chester zoo.

I don't know when Bannantyne had first laid eyes on the unfortunate hippo or when the idea came to him. I always imagine he had an epiphany but it might have occurred to him gradually, at first as whim and then as a consuming ambition. However it happened, Bannantyne started to make preparations for the arrival of the deceased hippo. I suppose that he had originally expected the hippo would pass away within the year. It was old and probably senile but it would stuff well.

There was a brief interlude during his preparations when a guinea pig called Pigsie arrived in his office. Tom, an Egyptologist who worked down the corridor, had been given his daughter's guinea pig to look after while she went away with her mother for a week's holiday. Sadly, Tom was not up to the job and the poor creature perished. Tom decided that the best thing to do was to deliver Pigsie to Bannentyne, more as an act of compassion for Bannantyne than any real desire to see it stuffed. The job was done adequately and with great relish but the end result was disturbing: Bannantyne had mounted Pigsie on a plinth, not in its usual round, contented position but in frozen animation, neck extended, two feet in mid-air. Needless to say Tom's daughter was horrified when, on coming home, she found Pigsie stuffed and mounted in mid-leap on her mantelpiece. Despite the contention, Pigsie was the nearest Bannantyne had been to the touch of warm flesh and it seemed to heighten his expectation about the hippo. But the hippo, blessed apparently by longevity or merely a desire not to be immortalised leaping – continued stubbornly to live.

I'm not too certain why anyone would voluntarily become a taxidermist. It has never been the ambition of any child that I have ever met and certainly, one assumes, anyone who wishes to spend their lives stuffing animals with straw or sawdust, or whatever they use nowadays, must have a sinister side to their character. I'm not saying that Bannatyne was sinister, don't imagine some white-coated man with bloodstained hands and Frankenstein laugh. In truth he was rather unmemorable and prone to bouts of depression. These became more acute with every month the hippo continued to flourish.

Eventually Bannantyne was driven to extreme measures – and he increasingly engaged his colleagues in discussions about the best way to dispatch a large mammal. No one really took him seriously – being cooped up in such a strange office surrounded by corpses would drive any man to such incoherent babbling. At the very point that Bannantyne decided on administering strychnine an Egyptologist took the bull by the horns – or the hippo by the ears – and rang the zoo to warn the zookeeper about the impending attempt on the hippo's life.

When Bannantyne arrived at the zoo, clutching his bottle of strychnine, several zookeepers followed him at a distance. I always imagine them armed with pitchforks but perhaps this would have been a little melodramatic. Bannantyne, contrary to expectations, paused a while and looked at the hippo, half submerged, as it chewed listlessly on a frond of vegetation and, after several minutes, he turned and walked away. I am told that Bannatyne handed in his notice to the museum the same day.

It was always a bit of a mystery but Tom, who had Pigsie sitting on his office bookshelf beside his ushabtis and steles, had a theory. Apparently Bannantyne realised, as he gazed at the hippo, that it was happy and content whilst he had never been. People gazed on it in much the same way as they gazed in on him in his claustrophobic office. It would have been cruel to kill the hippo. Bannantyne was the one who had been pickled and preserved, he had died from the inside out – years before.

I suppose that conversation with Tom helped me to hand in my notice and walk away from the museum in just the same way Bannantyne had done. I had never been happy there. I had been waiting for a hippo too, not literally like Bannantyne but metaphorically. It is easy to wait for hippos but infinitely better to realise the futility of it – before it is too late.

Kristy Kerruish

THE HIGH HOUSE

Only the illusion of wilderness here
where a dust-caked quarry nibbles at
the lower green slopes of a grey mountain and
weathered wooden signposts point to
the next stile,
and the next, and on
to ascending paths of compounded grit
(sacks of hardcore carried there
by quad-bikes), past ruined stone huts and
old mineral workings, the punctured sockets
of fenced-off holes; and so be made aware that
miners once trudged daily here
to enter the mountain. Above
come cairns,
walker's single stone added to stone and marking
bends in the much trodden route up
that hikers' soles — and in stretches running water —
have worn smooth through the rock,
to the one cairn
defining at last — heart thumping and breathing deep —
the peak.

And yet....
summit of a fell arrived at, as adventure it feels
artificial, does not allow
us to think of ourselves as either alone
or unique. But still....
on the way here
as we trod along a peaty hillside
birdsong speckled the morning mist that
lay in drifts across one valley
and separated the tops of some trees
from their trunks; and
as we tramped on up, and up,
resentful ewes went blundering off
through green and glistening bracken, leaving
fronds trembling drops of light;
and across the widening way were other sheep
in a line of white dashes
perforating a grey inverted fan of scree.
We came too upon a singular mass

53

of wisp-ended cloud cupped
in a brown mountain bowl, saw a rainbow
dripping silver into a lake....
And, at last, we arrived here
— to behold the western sea
aglitter with afternoon sunlight —
here, where we too feel that we belong
in Ivor Gurney's High House of Song.

Sam Smith

DARK PEAK

Already lost,
we hope it is a cairn.
Instead we find
a wing,
slanted to the sky,
its counter weight
immersed, emerging
from clouds of heather,
and the peat.

Only this.
A prop head. Twisted ribs.
The rest is long since gone,
picked clean by looters,
buried,
scattered
far across this high plateau,
broadcast in a blast
of scorched air
and shattered earth,
men and metal
screaming into
sudden, awful silence.

Only this.
Air loud with wind.
A lapis dome.
Deceptive sun.
Concealed bog.

And we stand apart,
with nothing to be said,
in awe only
of lives disintegrating here;
voices whipped away;
families sitting down to tea,
in Winnipeg or Perth,
around a quiet radio;
a bomber,
on a starless night,
all instruments gone,
dropping…

Ann Heath

55

A Breath of Fresh Air

As choking we emerged to sight, each blinking in the morning light,
Not thinking that we ever might have seen the sun again;
By the pit gates loved ones waited, praying to their God that fate would
Hand us back unharmed from hated Death in Hell's Domain;
Their ecstasy of dark relief these words cannot explain,
Nor bitter tears contain.

Two days before a hammer's spark ignited gas and lit the dark;
Those nearby saw flash and arc – their death quickly came;
From further off we heard a roar, then felt the rush of wind before
The intake ventilation door blew off in broiling flame;
The moments next are lost to me; I'll never ascertain
What happened as I'd lain.

Then as from some place distantly I heard the District Deputy
Whisper in my face as he screamed, "Was I blind or lame?"
We stumbled where the roof would sag and picked our feet through flesh
and rag
Collecting tallies for his bag, to give to each his name;
With every charred and dust-choked man as if in battle slain -
The Best of Houghton Main.

A photo sits upon my shelf; it's of the mine, the lads, myself,
Laughing, laiking, in full health before that shift, that day,
Reminding me of Hell and dust and till I join them that I must
Uphold their memory and trust – that is the Miner's Way;
To fail would be unthinkable – such brotherhood betrayed
Could never be repaid.

But in my dreams they didn't die; I drink with them; we fight; we cry;
I find it hard to justify the reason I was spared;
I walk the tips; I fish the streams – no more to sweat in four foot seams
But wonder what our short span means and offer up my prayer;
If only I could trade with them their peace for my despair
And a breath of my fresh air.

John Coopey

THE ABERFAN ROSE

Her mother found it near a holly tree,
A red rose growing in Aberfan,
Where the earth recited a black mass,
And inches between two friends in class
Meant life or death.

Some sat for hours at night
With their little black lamps by the graves
Remembering a hand through a crack in the wall
And horses with trams full of reddening ash,
A broken clock set at quarter to nine,
The fear of sleep when it rained.

And no one said sorry to Aberfan,
But community still came out of that void,
Weakening a time warp locked in grief
And people belonged to each other again.

Her younger sister goes there now
Where that rose still blooms in Aberfan,
But she won't pick a flower and shorten its life,
She watches it grow and wears its name.

Maggie Nicholls

TWIN TOWERS

An old friend stayed over the day after.
We went for a meal.
As usual we meandered through our past
remembered how we got boozed up at seventeen
two kids, full dressed in bed, pissed.
(What would parents have said ?)
Our lives hadn't been what we'd hoped
but we drank to the fact we'd survived.

We didn't mention the Towers
or the body scraps picked up
or the people who chose to jump
trying not to fall.

Angela Cooke

Spool the film back to the opening scene
where you enter the toilet and the man
follows you in. Listen to the screams
of the kids in the cinema as you stand

at the urinal and your heart's imitating
the noise of a clapperboard.
We need sound. What's the man saying?
Focus. Flick forward.

Remember you are the Director.
Don't be self-critical.
You told the ice-cream man you were sore
when he found you in the cubicle.

Don't edit the script.
You have to release this footage.
You're safe here. I am not a critic.
Don't stand off-stage.

You need to feature this event.
You have the lead part in a cast of two.
For fifty years you've censored this torment.
Don't leave! You're almost through.

Owen Gallagher

Forty Four Hundred Miles

You stand on that dusty, sand shaded roadside
in equilibrium with the free, wide air of
warm evenings by the swamp.
Familiar with the deep croaking and piquing chirps of nature, starting up
between
comfortable pauses
while you hang around for a ride
from the uncle who's never on time.

He pulls into the worn driveway between tin houses
rounding the collapsed chain fence,
spitting tobacco out the window and greeting you
with a lazy smile, everything done with the nonchalance
of those who know their place, who are accustomed
to the traditions of mosquito ridden nights
where you spend your time on the same roads and waters
of many a generation past
who were just like you.

When you climb into the jolty, metallic beast and the door
hammers shut
with the reverberation of a thousand repairs,
the engine charges with a gruff reminder that
wherever you're taken, be it
past the liquor-stained rest stop on the main stretch
out of town, or towards the abandoned barn on the outskirts
near the cemetery;
life here is assured.

The patterns you follow are as set as the grazing of the malnourished
cattle.
The dull ringing of a cow's bell echoes
in the darkness of another sweltering night.
You try to sleep, thinking of what you can do tomorrow
that you haven't yet done,
or if that's even possible.

Ryan Bowd

The TB Test 1985

The best way to get to know a country area
is to go with a rural vet on farm visits

MARDI GRAS
FIRST NIGHT IN NEW ORLEANS

(i)

After honking traffic on Canal Street:
loud rap from the yellow Cadillac, pulsing
like a bullfrog; walking through crowds
on Bourbon Street, catching blasts of music:
disco, jazz, blues from doorways of bars
and strip-joints; after Hurricanes
at O'Brien's and a bottle of Ferrari-Carano
at Oyster Bar, the evening lights up
in the glow of the restaurant's golden
pumpkin lamps, the amber flame of cognac;
find ourselves on Rue Royale along with
the wedding procession waving white handkerchiefs
in rhythm with the band; entwined we slow-dance
to the sound of the jazz saxophone blowing in from the river.

(ii)

Don't remember gunfire -
sirens, blue lights flashing
and red tape fluttering
    across the sidewalk, just
    a block from our hotel.

Marion Ashton

As if, hidden somewhere in the city,
someone nursing a festering grudge
just lifted a black-faced scarecrow doll
from its red silk, seven-inch box, tucked
a tuft of coarse dark hair under its straw
cloth armpit, stuck a silver pin in its neck,
then three more into the belly and the backs
of both knees, causing her to jerk
a stone-eyed face, clutch a cramping gut,
to gag, stagger and knock into groups
of grinning tourists, all reaching
skyward, trying to catch the flung
strings of carnival beads, falling gold-
purple-green from wrought-iron balconies.

Marion Ashton

BLUE HAT

A few snaps of street-lamp shadows on Brennans' pink wall,
and suddenly I'm Cartier Bresson-Robert Doisneau
rolled into one: several shots of flaking paint layers
on a horse-head hitching-post, a courtyard fountain
viewed through the cornstalk fence of 915 Royale,
Cajun, Voodoo and Carnival signs caught in a single
frame, a street player's battered euphonium, leftover
tails of Mardi Gras tinsel fluttering from a balcony.

The picture of the girl in the crumpled hat with red ribbons
is a back view; she's sitting on her heels at the kerbside
next to a pink bicycle: an art student maybe, going for
the bo-ho-chic look: a cornflower blue silk blouse,
canvas shoes and the vintage net petticoat worn as a skirt.
Walking by, the view from the front is a grey-haired,
raddled old woman, muttering to herself, loose-skin hands
sifting the trash-can contents of a plastic Walmart bag.

Marion Ashton

SUNDAY MORNING

Behind the padlocked gates
of Jackson Square Gardens,
slow-paced workers swab
Saturday night's excesses
off the walkways,
hose down blowsy banks

of pink azaleas, open-throated
in the rising heat.
From *Desire's* doorway,
a shock of lemon Lycra:
a teenage girl blinks
into the sun-slap glare, clatters

down *Chartres* as if
in someone else's stilettos,
loose bra-strap slipping
off the shoulder: a surrender
of tired white lace
across smooth, black flesh.

Marion Ashton

TAROT

He thinks it will be the same as all the other times:
he'll take me to Muriel's and we'll sit at the best
table in the Gris Gris Room. There'll be champagne
and orchids, chandelier lights glinting in his eyes.
He'll smile and smile, explain those receipts,
the unexpected nights away. I'll watch him slide
oysters along his tongue, bite into snapper flesh,
lick sauce from his lips. He'll pick the moment
to push a small blue box across the table – diamond
bangle or a fat-stone ring. And his final flourish:
that slow deal of dollars from the thick casino wad.

He doesn't know I've been to see the Tarot boy –
the gifted one - who looked me in the eye, smiled,
nodded before I even turned a card, knowing,
just like I knew, this time would be different.

Marion Ashton

People rarely split up on good terms. If they're not busy seeing who can empty the joint bank account the fastest, then they're busy working their way sexually through a slew of your friends and acquaintances. As much as we protest and pretend, we are still at heart very much the petulant child who demanded sweeties whenever sweeties came into view.

Becky and Bob's relationship was no exception to the rule.

The breaking point of their courtship could be traced back to a stroll in the park, when Becky, arm in arm and very much in love at that moment, spied a rival female approaching her and her beau.

We use 'rival' lightly however. Mentally, and we use the word 'mentally' not as lightly in this case, she viewed all women as rivals, threats and potential succubus.

As the potential 'scarlet woman' passed them by, Becky let out a small bark, not dissimilar to the noise made by a Chihuahua or similar breed of small dog.

Though this wasn't an unusual thing for Becky to do, it was the first time her boyfriend had ever been present to witness it. After a few more paces, Bob stopped and asked her if he was correct in thinking that she had just barked. Becky smiled and nodded, laughing it off as one of her numerous quirks and eccentricities.

Bob was all for quirks. He was also not averse to the occasional eccentricity but barking at strangers? This was maybe a quirk too far.

The word amicable, derived from the Latin word for 'friend' is most commonly used in conjunction with the end of a relationship. It's more likely to be found preceding horrible words like divorce, breakup or split than say, pet purchase, cheesecake or nil-nil draw.

By adding this magic word, we believe we are making the following word less horrible and creating the illusion that it's a joint decision, though one of them has clearly decided before the other to amicably destroy their relationship outright.

Bob had never had to break up with anyone; it usually just happened and rarely was it amicably. Not that Bob was a bad boyfriend. The various indiscretions Bob had destroyed relationships with, in no particular order, included putting the toilet roll on the holder the wrong way round, not wiping the underside of the toilet seat and not being made of the pliable clay that some women seem to think they can fashion their ideal man from. Women may say they want a tall, dark stranger but what they really mean is an impeccably toilet trained one.

Bob was a firm believer in bending. In all relationships you have to bend otherwise you will eventually snap. Becky's barking was a step too far. What was next? Urinating on him to mark her territory? He was not willing or European enough to wait and find out.

Choosing the local train station as a mid-way meeting point to end their relationship, Bob thought he had all bases covered.

After he had explained how it was him and not her, that they would always be friends and he would never forget her, Bob thought it had all gone rather well.

Becky after initial tears and a volley of expletives, decided to get on with her life. She also decided, while she was at it she would do her very best to destroy his. She soon realised this was rather silly, if not immature, so decided to destroy his future instead.

Bob awoke one morning, nearly a month to the day he had ended his dalliance with Becky, fresh from a dream that had been forgotten before it had even been recalled. He stretched, yawned before padding downstairs in search of a hearty breakfast of chocolate flavoured puffed rice and a black coffee with five sugars.

As Bob sat in front of the television, stuffing cereal into his face while his coffee conspired to dissolve his teeth, there was a knock at the door.

Ever the gentleman, Bob left his mother to answer the door while he shovelled mouthfuls of soft, brown mush into his face. A dribble of chocolate milk ran down his chin and onto the Sex Pistols t-shirt he slept in.

Bob's mother walked in carrying a box. She placed it on the sofa next to him and quickly rattled off the reasons why young men shouldn't ride motorcycles, as they were all death traps, before disappearing back into the kitchen.

Bob was not expecting a delivery, let alone a motorcycle helmet, so studied the label that had been crudely taped to its outside. Written in a spidery hand he didn't recognise was his name and address.

He shook the box lightly and something moved inside. After all, the way his mother had huffed and puffed bringing it into the room suggested the box was clearly not empty, so surely something had to be inside it.

The box had at some point already been opened. Brown tape had been inexpertly applied over the clear tape that had originally sealed it. Bob shrugged and dragged his thumbnail over the tape, attempting to break the seal.

Bob had spent the last few years working at a bookstore. Whilst working there he had been told a tale by a workmate called Dave. He had regaled Bob with a tale about his older brother and his former girlfriend, whom one Valentine's Day had sent him a pig's heart in a velvet lined box. Whilst some people would have regarded the note which read 'I could not give you my own heart so this will have to do' as an amazingly romantic gesture, Dave's brother when hit with the stench of a pig's decomposing heart was only struck by a wave of nausea. Once this had passed, he got on the phone and ended their dalliance.

While Bob could happily recount this story to anyone he drunkenly encountered around Valentine's Day, nothing prepared him for what he would find inside his box.

For inside his box was Becky's mummified head. Slightly shrunken, expertly embalmed and without any doubt her real, actual head.

He didn't know why he had calmly folded the flaps of the box shut again, carefully placing his half-eaten bowl of cereal to one side and then proceeded to take the box upstairs to his bedroom.

His mind would have raced with a million thoughts but it just raced with one. It wasn't even a thought and his young mind had already reduced it to the appropriate textspeak of WTF.

The box remained unremarkable compared with its gruesomely fascinating contents. It didn't smell any worse than the faint odour of the embalming fluid its contents had been preserved with and hadn't leaked any fluid, either preservative or bodily based. In fact, Bob had started to feel so at ease with what he imagined the box had contained, he had started to doubt himself, believing himself to be the victim of some elaborate hoax.

No matter how much he tried to convince himself that inside the box was nothing more than maybe a very realistic papier-mâché head, Bob still couldn't muster the courage to look inside the box again.

Bob was deciding between phoning the police or taking another peek inside the box when his mobile phone started ringing. The call, according to his phone, was from Becky.

He stared at the phone blankly as her name, spelt all in capitals, glowed from the green screen of his old Nokia. The ringtone, Kick, repeated itself three more times before his answer phone kicked in. Bob at this time of the morning was neither ready to receive calls from either the dead or possible murderers.

The phone had other ideas though and was soon ringing again. It would be only a matter of time before his mother complained about the noise.

Bob considered turning the phone off but since he had never seen anyone do that in a horror film, decided his best course of action was to answer it. After all, a man needs to know where he stands in situations such as these.

The call was from neither the dead nor a murderer but from Becky's mum. She quickly explained that if he knew what was best for him, he would show the box to no one and wait for her to call again in a couple of days' time. If he were to show the contents of the box to anyone, he would soon experience a life changing turn of events. From her tone, it didn't sound like it would be a good one.

Bob didn't have a clue what to do.

A few days passed. Bob had even managed to wangle some short notice leave from his employers as he patiently waited by the phone. Thankfully, as he had not left the house since receiving his gruesome parcel, his mother hadn't had the opportunity to nosey into his box yet. Yet was a very apt word, as she was the kind of nosey old woman who got into everything. There were renowned cat burglars and ninjas who were in awe of her stealth like abilities.

Bob was sat in front of the television chewing a piece of toast when he finally received a text message from Becky's phone. It read, 'BECKY WANTS 2 C U'. He quickly composed a reply asking when they could meet, eschewing the caps lock format her mother had used. He assumed it was her mother; after all, it was only the elderly who couldn't work out such things as not writing everything in capitals.

As he got himself dressed, he mused over whether to take the head with him or leave it in his room, risking his mother's insatiable need to stick her beak into everything within her domain. It wasn't a hard decision, the box would have to come with him.

Stood on her doorstep, box under his arm, Bob knocked on his ex-girlfriend's front door. The door was quickly answered by her mother, who ushered him into a cigarette smoke filled living room. A collection of ceramic houses, tastefully arranged in a glass cabinet stood besides the door to the kitchen. It was the only thing he remembered from his last and now he thought about it, only visit to her house.

Her mother looked tired. The kind of tired reserved for women who will never catch up with the sleep they have lost. A tiredness that no amount of early nights, expensive creams or lie-ins could ever put right.

There was no chit-chat. She sat herself in a chair on the other side of the room and lit a cigarette, fixing him with a hateful stare. She smoked the longer variation of cigarette referred to as Superkings due to their 100mm length and not down to any preference dictated by super-power endowed monarchs.

He watched her inhale a lungful of smoke, not breaking her hateful gaze. The room felt far too hot.

As she flicked her ash into a large, green glass ashtray there was the sound of movement from upstairs. Her mother broke her stare and glanced at the Artexed ceiling as the footsteps shuffled along the corridor above and towards the landing.

She stubbed her cigarette out with enough anger to release a flurry of burning tobacco skywards and got to her feet. She mumbled something about how he was lucky to even talk to her and if she had it her way, he would've been left with it, whatever 'it' may be. She then stormed out of the room and into the garden to smoke more cigarettes.

Bob didn't know what to expect and couldn't disguise the fear he felt as whatever was supposed to be his former girlfriend Becky lumbered down the stairs.

When she entered the room, head still very much intact and attached, she looked as shocked as he was to see him sat there. After a few moments of awkward silence, she stormed outside and had a brief but heated discussion with her mother. Much pointing and swearing ensued. She soon returned, flopping into the seat her mother had recently vacated.

Besides the new looks of intense hatred he was encountering, Bob could not help but notice how fresh her face looked and what looked like the reddening that recently healed scars had that encircled her neck.

There was no easy way to start the conversation. Bob's hand rested on top of the box. Becky crossed her arms under her bosom and scowled.

He said she looked well. Becky sneered a sneer so dripping with hate and resentfulness it defied both similes and clever metaphors. It was what it was. She had gone past despising him, past hating him but worst of all past caring less than even one iota for him.

It was the iotas that counted, the jots, the tittles and Becky counted none of them. She was steadfast in her resolve.

Becky quickly explained that her severed head was his penance for breaking her heart and he was to bear it for the rest of his life or until the day that she decided they were even. If he attempted to dispose of it, she would disappear and he would spend the rest of his life behind bars. She had cut off her head to spite her ex.

Oh he begged and he pleaded but his words fell on ears as deaf as the ones inside his box. She insisted the box must remain in his ownership until the day she saw fit to release him from her macabre contract. She made no effort to suppress her smile. She and she alone would decide when they were even.

Bob sat in the library and read about spiders regenerating legs, starfish re-growing arms and lizards growing new tails. He read about flatworms being cut in two to become two separate worms. He pored over articles about sharks re-growing teeth and sea cucumbers when cut into pieces, the bits each becoming a new sea cucumber. Becky however was not a sea cucumber.

He had no idea what she was.

So the box returned home with Bob. Home to where his inquisitive mother would sooner than later look inside the box and find what she would assume was a grizzly trophy. Who knows what she would do?

Bob started to pack.

Many, many years later, the police were called to the bedsit of the quiet man who lived at the end of the hall, when the smell got too strong for his neighbours to ignore any longer. After the landlord had been unable to open the door because of the mountain of junk mail that held it firmly shut, the police had broken it down with a ram normally reserved for drugs raids. His former neighbours loitered in the corridors, rubbernecking.

They gossiped to one another about how the man had kept himself to himself, rarely receiving visitors bar the girl with the scar that encircled her neck who occasionally stopped by. They questioned his sexuality due to his lack of other lady callers and his general mental health. They invented and fabricated tales about his reluctance to leave his room besides from when he left for work, always with the same battered cardboard box slung under his arm. They mused and meditated, concocted and invented as his body was carried past them, zipped up inside a black body bag.

The police soon left and the landlord pulled the door shut, though it remained un-lockable as it had been nearly wrenched from its hinges. It was mere minutes before a small group of inquisitive souls decided to have a sneaky look round.

Bedsits are depressing. When your whole life can be contained in one, maybe two rooms and a shared bathroom, your life has clearly gone awry somewhere along the way.

The assembled rag-tag group of residents stood in Bob's doorway. Some eyeing items they could purloin for their own meagrely furnished rooms, others just wanting to satisfy their morbid curiosity.

A couple of them broke off from the main group and approached the old box that sat on the coffee table. The box was dead centre. The tape that held it shut had been opened and then reapplied on many an occasion. The box would've been right in front of him when he expired. A dark stain marked the spot where Bob had been peeled from the sofa.

They tore through the tape with the aid of a key and pulled the flaps wide. They looked at one another in mild confusion and then back into the box.

The box was of course nearly empty, except for a bright yellow post-it note that had been stuck to the very bottom of the box. On it, printed in neat handwriting were four words.

Tom Dixon

THREE MONTHS AFTER WRITING BECAME CURRENCY

Poets clamber up Ben Nevis, pen in hand, to savour the sunrise,
passing broken-down playwrights who've surged all night
and now clutch this month's rent.

Nocturnal novelists stagger from bedsits and loft-apartments,
blinking into noon-applauses and answerless questions,
to deposit years of ramblings in their broken banks
and slam mortgage applications on managers' desk.

Grammarians and librarians emerge from dusty shelves to form the
Plagiarism Police, proofreading the treasury's coffers and conducting
door to door literary evaluations,
lining the House of Commons and leading debates on the Oxford
Comma.

London's Shard brims with Romantics as emergency editors pick at
American imports,
leafed through by distraught Canary Wharf-ers, pacing through the deals
in their minds:
two tons of assorted Byron for a truckload of Ginsberg's Howl.

Creativity manuals are handed out, as school bells ring to nobody
and youths lie in circles on Glastonbury Tor, noting changes in clouds
and tugging at the heads of daisies.

After months of bobbing at sea, Icelandic crews of cod trawlers queue on
the dockside,
and dragging crates of sagas, stagger on the steady land to the closest
bars,
where they drink volcanic black ale and list rhymes for fire and ice.

Sam Kemp

THE MOROCCAN DRUM

She hoisted the drum up on her shoulder again
where the raggedy strap mingled with the narrow
one of her smart black top, while the sudden
cold breeze washed over her bare skin.

This was not going to deter her, so she stood
taller with her head at an angle to defy anyone
thinking she was stupid, including herself.

She had searched so hard to get the right drum
this one she even got at a good price after haggling.

Being dusty she washed it, as it dried the skin
cracked. Was it worth the effort to bring it home?

Yes she would bring it back. On route
she left it behind a couple of times, as if she
wasn't quite sure, it was retrieved by kind people.

Standing in queues strangers affirmed her
decision despite the crack which to each in turn
she pointed out. On through check after check
back to Ireland, where the drum now sits in silence
while the recipient tries his skills on a guitar.

Eliza Dear

THE DEAR OLD THINGS

There is a market for old things,
a seller's market, down-at-heel
brown furniture and obsolete
white goods. The hagglers hover in
the wings, and we appreciate
like bone-rich stock or blood-thick wine,
dear old things that served their time,
or gimcrack things not meant to last

that somehow did, outpurposing
utility. Priceless perhaps,
at any rate unpriceable,
we linger in corners in the new
temples to storage out beside
the motorway in air-conditioned
bliss, where no dust is allowed to
settle on us, nor any spider weave.

Terence Dooley

LÈCHE-VITRINES

The light is fading from the shopping street
in a chichi town, in Northern France.
The road is cobbled and slopes steeply down:
the low light strikes the cobbles like a field
of gold. In the deep drains a rushing sound
drowns out the silver ice-pick of late heels.
The cubical vitrines are intricate
with rich displays of edibles, or stuffs
sumptuous to the eye and fancied touch.
The grilles are coming down, and we can lick
the frosted windows till we meet the gaze
of the proprietor and freeze, tongue-tied.
Price-tags are blank, but if you need to ask...

Years pass, and, having striven, we could stride
into the warm boutique like carriage folk
and point to what we want, then realise
we do not want it now, but something else:
the hunger for the thing we couldn't have
back then. Below the shops, the street
swerves out of sight, and the sky above seems
brighter there, as though reflecting water
inexpensive, and quite drinkable

Terence Dooley

MALE

I think I shall not buy a gun,
    for fear that I might use it:
    that it might spit forth
    like a penis
    like an opinion
    like a belief in god.

I think I am man enough.

Graham Buchan

FLOOD 2

The river flows down the street now.
It bubbles up through tarmac,
Slips over shop steps, celebrating,
Barges into doorways,
Creates dark, slopping pools in cellars.
Rats discover new platforms.
Chewing turds they mutter among themselves
Tasting disorder, this perilous turnaround:
The mangled glass, the shifting of wood
And look in the supermarkets! Look up!
See the flimsy roof and girders
Where pigeons roost.
Have they never been much more than cheap jerry sheds
Harbouring stores in temporary tins and cardboard?
And what is this mania for scattering?
Everything is so dispersed!
Cars, bottles, office chairs, clothes hangers;
As if litter doesn't matter any more,
Is no longer a crime.
The rats shake their heads, hop over sand bags,
Make fine novel fortresses
In places once forbidden.

Clive Donovan

Seeing What Isn't There

Forty years since I was here.
They have built, too much perhaps,
still not enough to make it modern.
I see no change.

A South Bank terrace
that was half as wide, at least,
watches Gherkin, Shard, Eye.
I see no change.

On the Tube: at each station
pseudopods of citizens,
hurried, harried,
rush the same pavements, crossings, doors.
I see no change.

Later, Carnac:
where youthful unknown Stonehenge,
Forum, Alp, inspired and chilled,
does not impress with travelogue familiarity.

I wonder if memory refuses to see,
release what it thinks it knows,
or diminished by too much information,
we see nothing with our own eyes?
How can we ever be surprised?

Grahaeme Barrasford Young

Larnax, embossed with a perfect celestial star,
yolky gold, glowing emblem of the Temenids
descended directly from the Gods.

Within the quiet chamber, delicate diadems
forged from sunlight. Tiny laurel leaves for high birth
and myrtle flowers, symbol of immortality.

Silence. Gold and ivory couches, silver ladles, cups,
amphoras brimming wine. Plates of figs, olives, cassia
moulding. Persephone's fate in faded paint.

She waits for her guests, deep in the underworld,
with libations for the dead. The powerful, the beautiful
drawn by the sleek stallions, jewelled and bridled.

Purified by fire, great King, encircled by weapons: his sword
greaves, iron helmet, shield. His ash wears an oak wreath.
He lies inside his chamber, held in this metallic womb.

When they break through, centuries have stacked in the gloom:
great wedges of dust, crumbling stone, warped iron nails.
The faint shrieking of horses, screaming from the flames.

Khadija Rouf

Mr. Smith with his favorite dog,
Woldgate Bridlington, 1981 (version 2)

DUSK

Seen from the other side
everything looks different:
the lighted lamp on the kitchen sill,
half an IKEA cushion
and the corner of an easy chair;
a son's first suit hanging
in the bedroom doorway
with its pockets waiting
to be unpicked and beyond it
the gleaming banisters
and the stairs. I'm looking
through lighted windows
into someone else's life.
It looks calmer than mine,
more self-assured, and yet
the books are the same,
it's the same brand of tea
and that's my blue and white
spotted jug a stranger's
filled with cornflowers
and sweet peas. Any moment now
she's going to reach for the kettle
or glance into the garden
where I'm hovering like a moth,
half attracted to the light.

Ruth Sharman

LOVELY LEITRIM

Mother banned me from singing Irish rebel songs
    when Shergar was kidnapped by the IRA.
'Connolly and the Easter leaders must be saddling up,'

she said. 'If these imposters are not reined in,
    no legged creature will be safe.'
Every horse in the Republic was confined to quarters.

Rifles and pitchforks were kept ready.
    The patron saint for animals was exhausted
with requests. Back street bookies took bets.

Clairvoyants, psychics and diviners were unable
    to fathom the whereabouts of this colt
whose retirement was filled with mares queuing to foal.

The ransom went unpaid. Mother, her face a fury, said,
    'The cheek of these bog men to shoot a horse
you'd swear had eight legs, not a turf's throw

from my old home in Ballinamore. Will you quieten
    my nerves son, and sing Lovely Leitrim,
and put a pound on Her Rags to win at Ayr.'

Owen Gallagher

GLASS

On behalf one belief or another
more towns - was Chechnya then Homs -
will be rendered windowless

    No domestic goddess
    will cope
    with this amount of dust

Streets will become passages
through pushed-aside rubble
around the freshest craters

Somewhere unseen
will be the magpie chatter
of small arms fire

That's on the telly now:
we are a people made fearful
by newspapers and hourly bulletins

and who know too much of too little -
                some symptoms
                of some illnesses

Here now
the most distressing sound and sight
beyond late summer's open windows
is the cacophonous lament of searching ewes

as they crowd together
through field gateways
their lambs been carted off to slaughter

Sam Smith

HE TURNED THE WORLD AROUND

He turned the world around,
or so they told him
and those he brought back with him
in small mementos;
a tobacco pouch, a cap badge
a practised silence.

The day he came home
he asked for matches,
stripped naked in the garden
and burnt his uniform,
lice encrusted seams
crackling in the flames.

He spent the rest of his days
in the night of the mine,
spitting coal dust, bent
under the weight of fossils,
Derbyshire coal tattooing his back
with small cuts and chips.

In the evenings
he brought order to the garden;
ranks of cabbages marked out
with string, runner beans
bound tidily to canes,
raspberries safely netted

and in the drawing stillness,
when he heard the chime
of the kettle on the hob,
he would pause to fill his pipe
feeling the worn leather of the pouch,
staring at the white lines of leeks.

Ilse Pedler

MANDELSTAM

The light dust is darkened
Under the streetlights
In the middle of the night.

Only my eyes touch
The long moment that my fingers feel and my ears hear:
The last pulse of warmth
And the eternal sound.

A cold night –
But still the soft reaching crackle of flames
Conjures Arabia,
A strange slow sleepiness of time.

Cold cat,
Your delicate skull smashed,
Laid dead by a drain;
The dark cars pass, their headlights blinding.

The light dust is darkened;
A black-and-white cat whispering
Words less than nothing
Passes on that …

And the Phoenix speaks with the voice of Stalin.

William Alderson

AT PRESENT

If I am asked, and with a moment's thought,
without a time-piece, I can speak the time.
It seems, in some respects, a useless gift,
but I set store by it, to know when now is
waking from a dream, or yet adrift
on endless afternoons, a castaway.
I am the minute-hand, I am the hours,
the arms akimbo or the arms across,
the trembling digit in fluorescent green
that will not change forever, and then will
spill over like a silent waterfall,
and, if you ask me for my reckoning,
among the many moments there have been,
I count back to the time I saw you last.

Terence Dooley

It was a Saturday morning and Mum and Terry were at it again in the kitchen. Nothing had been thrown or broken yet but the voices were getting louder. I was sitting with Jay in the living room, watching him play Destiny on his PS3.

'What's it about this time?' I said to Jay.

He didn't look at me. 'The same thing it's always about,' he said. 'Your mum.'

'It's not always her fault,' I said.

'Yes it is,' said Jay. 'You're twelve years old - what do you know?'

'He asks for it sometimes,' I said. 'He makes it happen.'

Jay turned to me, his eyes glistening. 'Say that again,' he said, 'and I will break your face.'

'I'm going out,' I said.

'Good,' said Jay.

It was sunny outside but it can be colder than it looks so I went and got my old coat from under the stairs. I put my woolly hat on, too. Then I went out through the back door so Mum and Terry wouldn't see me leave.

I hadn't really thought about where I was going until I was halfway down our street. I just didn't want to be in the house anymore. But I knew some of the kids from school played football in the park on Saturday mornings so I decided to go there. I could watch them play. I might even get myself invited into a game.

I never made it to the park, though, because that was when I met her. She was sitting on a bus shelter bench with her head in her hands, crying. She had a red leather jacket on over a black dress. She was wearing black tights and there was a pair of red high heels lying on their sides by her feet. I was going to walk past her but something made me stop and she must have known I was there because she suddenly took her hands from her face and looked up at me. She had dark brown hair and her eyes were dark, too. Her lips were painted red like the jacket and shoes. There were black streaks down her face where her make-up had run, but even messed up like that I thought she was the most beautiful woman I had ever seen. 'Who the hell are you?' she said.

'Nobody,' I said.

'Everybody's somebody,' she said. 'I don't suppose you have any tissues on you?'

I checked my pockets. 'No.'

'I seem to have used all of mine up, what with all this crying,' she said. 'Perhaps I'll stop. It never helps anyway, does it?' Then she burst into tears again.

I took my woolly hat off and handed it to her. 'You can use this if you like,' I said. 'It's clean.'

She took it off me and dabbed at her face with it. Then she put it on as if it was hers now. 'You're a very kind young man,' she said. 'How old are you?'

'Fourteen,' I said.

'Fourteen,' she said. 'Imagine that. Now would you like to help me find my car? I seem to have lost it.'

'How can you lose a car?' I said.

'That,' she said, 'is very simple. You go to a town you have never been to before, to meet a man you have never met before. You park in some anonymous backstreet. You sit in your car on your own getting very drunk, because you think it makes you wittier and more attractive, then you ask a faceless passer-by to direct you to the bar where you're meeting the man. You meet the man and you get even more drunk with him and then you go to a club with him and then you go back to his place. He turns out to be an absolute tosser who incidentally claims not to have even heard of the street you parked your car in, you end up at half past four in the morning telling him to go fuck himself because he's certainly not fucking you, and voila! Excuse my French.'

'And what *was* the name of the street you left your car on?' I asked.

'I can't remember now, can I?' she said. 'Hope Street?'

'I've never heard of Hope Street,' I said. 'I think it probably isn't that.'

'I'm sure you're right,' she said. 'What's your name, anyway?'

'Stephen,' I said.

'Well, Stephen,' she said, 'are you going to help me?'

'If you like,' I said. 'Can you remember anything at all about the street? Was there anything near it that I might know?'

'You mean like a landmark?' she said. 'No, it was just a street. It was terraced houses on both sides, though, and I guess it wasn't far from the town centre.'

'Were you really that drunk?' I said.

'Oh, yes,' she said, 'I was very drunk indeed.' She reached down for the red high heels and then stood up, with the shoes in one hand and her handbag in the other. 'Lead on, Macduff,' she said.

'OK,' I said, and we started walking.

She had nothing on her feet but her tights and after a while I said, 'Doesn't it hurt, walking without shoes?'

She looked at me as though I'd asked her something really personal. Then she said, 'Yes, it hurts. But it hurts wearing the heels too. And my flat shoes are in the car.'

I thought to myself that maybe the high heeled shoes were like the drinking - they made her feel more attractive. 'Perhaps you'll start to recognise things when we get nearer to the centre of town,' I said. 'Do you remember anything from when you drove in?'

She stopped walking then, and she looked at me and said, 'The truth is, Stephen, I was already drunk. I'd had half a bottle of vodka before I even got into my car. What do you think of that?'

'It is what it is,' I said.

'That's a very grown up sounding thing to say,' she said, looking at me harder now. 'Where have you picked that up from?'

'It's something my mum says.'

'I see,' she said, and we started walking again.

When we were near the end of the road she started asking me about school. She wanted to know which GCSEs I was doing. I'm not doing any yet but I told her it was just the usual ones, Maths and English and whatever, and she seemed to believe me.

'I never did very well at school, Stephen,' she said. 'I didn't really try. But I could have done well if I'd wanted to.'

'So what do you do now?' I said.

'When I'm not getting drunk and losing myself in strange towns, you mean?'

'I suppose.'

'I'm an actress,' she said.

'Have you been in any films?'

'Probably none that you'll have seen.'

'Have you been on the telly?'

'Sort of,' she said. 'Look, Stephen, do you mind if we talk about something else?' We were at the junction now, opposite the park gates. I could see the kids playing football. 'Left or right?' she said.

'Left,' I said. 'Do you recognise anything yet?'

'Not a thing,' she said. 'But at least I'm not crying anymore, am I? That's got to be good, hasn't it?'

'Yes,' I said. I looked down at her feet. I wondered what she would say if I offered her my trainers. 'Why were you crying anyway?'

'Oh, because of everything,' she said. 'Because of what my life has come to. You know, I think I'm going to have to put these shoes on after all.' She stopped walking again and held her handbag out for me to hold. I could tell that her feet were beginning to really hurt her now but I didn't say anything about my trainers.

She put the heels on and straightened herself up with a strange little smile. It was then that I realised why I hadn't mentioned my trainers. It was because I wanted to see her in the heels. I passed her handbag back to her and we carried on.

It wasn't long then before things started to come back to her. First it was a mouthwash advert on the hoardings near the old bus station. She definitely remembered seeing that, she said. Then it was the taxi office on the corner. But she couldn't remember whether she had seen them when she was driving into town the night before, or later on when she was walking to the bar. 'Or,' she said, suddenly looking like she might cry again, 'it might even have been this morning.'

I was listening to her carefully, trying my best to help, and I led her through the Market Place towards where I thought her car might be. But there were a lot of things I wanted to ask her and I knew my time was running out. Why had she gone to meet that man? What had they fallen out about? Did she know how beautiful she was? If I was older, would I at least have a chance? I didn't want to ask her about the acting anymore, though. I knew enough about that now.

In the end we found her car halfway down Long Street and I hadn't asked her anything. The car was an old silver Peugeot, a bit dented here and there but still quite nice really. She unlocked it and opened the front passenger door. Her flat shoes were lying in the footwell, just like she'd said, along with an empty vodka bottle. She lowered herself sideways onto the seat with her legs stretching out onto the pavement and changed her shoes. I could see the pink soles of her feet where her tights had worn through. 'I still have your hat on, Stephen,' she said, suddenly.

'You can keep it if you like,' I said.

'In case I start crying again?'

92

'I suppose.'

'Well,' she said.

I wanted to ask her not to go. Or to take me with her. Or something.

She got up out of the car and passed me my hat. 'Well,' she said again. 'Should I give you a lift back?'

I nearly said yes, because I wanted to be in the car with her. But I knew it was no use. 'I'll walk,' I said.

She closed the passenger door then she gave me a big hug and kissed me on the cheek. I could feel her boobs pressing against my chest. I wanted to put my arms around her but they just hung at my sides. 'You're going to remember me, Stephen,' she said. Then she let me go. Then she got in her car and drove away and I never saw her again.

Except that I do still see her, in my dreams. Because in my dreams I get in the car with her and we go off together. We leave everything and everyone behind us. We leave Mum and Terry and Jay and that man in town and all those men she was an actress with and all the men making the videos. We're in our own movie now. We're on a road trip, on the longest road you could ever imagine, just driving and driving. She has one hand on the steering wheel and the other is resting on my leg and we're in love. Her red high heels are lying by my feet and I know that when we get there she'll put them on for me. No one understands it except us, but that doesn't matter. It is what it is.

Gregory Heath

First, a deluge. Smallbrook is a raging torrent.

Black lambs, with springs in their feet, are bursting with the excitement of it all.

A windblown cherry comes down in a shower of blossom and shattered limbs. The fence is in tatters.

Over Dartmoor the clouds press low. But Cornwall ends its day in a crimson blaze.

Gangs of bare-legged Launceton girls try to look cool in heels too high for them. Boy gangs loiter.

The swallows are back. Shearwaters of the inshore, their waves the rolling corn.

Salt laden storms blow in overnight. The sheep are in a heap under the hedge.

Low tide on the Tresillian. Shellduck and little egrets fly in.

In the end, the sun shines on Padstow. "...and happy are those little birds and the merrier we will sing ..."

And summer begins.

Julie Baber

TAR BALLS

Each ball was a tangle of rags
Soaked in tar, every inch Brer Rabbit's
babies, single string clackers
tied with farm wire to a twisted handle,
held at arm's length, swung to and fro
then higher and overhead
so the centrifugal force
kept the fire from flares and dirndls.

Three streams of flame flowed,
halos of light, from The Lamb,
the scout hut and Taplins farm.
The turning torches converged
at the green across from the church
towards the house-high stack
of wind-fall branches and old pallets
in a procession of glowing faces.

The wranglers circled the bonfire,
still curving their tar balls in the air.
One by one fire-balls flew
some to the heart, some to the head
some became incoming missiles
to the crowd opposite the thrower,
hastily collected in asbestos gloves,
returned to the conflagration.

Villagers would warm their hands,
scoff sausages doused with onions,
hunker down on bales of straw
made sofa-like by farmers' lads,
sup pints or halves of tepid beer,
watch the young girls cadging
firemen's lifts and engine rides,
wander off to sing in pub snugs.

But Charlie Hayes is gone ten years,
filled St John's with paid respects.
His farm split into developments
and no one makes tar balls like him.
The village is mostly stockbrokers

who adore the traditional
but don't want the green disfigured
by a charred circle through the winter.

Sue Spiers

SPARROWHAWK

Sinewed yellow claws
  grip the splintered arm of wood
    on the rotting garden bench.

She spreads each wing
  to show a matador's cloak
    of russet, sand and cream

as the fierce beak grasps
  every barb in turn
    to be rhythmically preened.

She breathes a birthright sun
    down to the bone;

subdues the mown grass,
  the cultivated roses,
    those invaders of her kingdom.

Every strand of every feather's
    groomed by hunger

ready for the rapid flight
  through hawthorn, holly, gorse,
    the sudden snatch and kill.

Jean Stevens

LOCH NA KEAL

And consider the buzzard.
It casts no shadow
on the obsidian skin

of Loch Na Keal.
Watch how it strives
against the wind,

how its wings plot
an unlikely course
above Ben More,

how the wind
takes the *hing*
of its voice,

ushers it
across the loch.
Look at the hooded crows,

usually so quick
to mob raptors
at will;

Today, they are not
so cocksure
of themselves.

Look at how
They cower
In the trees?

If you are the buzzard,
your troubles are the crows
and here, now, on this day,

they just might leave you alone.

Mark Connors

HEDGEGROW

A Scouser and neighbour John Owen
And myself set grisselenia fairly soon

As we moved into our houses
It took ages to grow - we manured it

It was green and clean and homely
Easily cut once or twice a year

Hired a professional - difficult
Enough to simply keep the grass down

Now I have the back problems
My mama still lives thankfully

The bind weed or Robin run
The hedge has taken over

Call on good neighbour
Joe, order a standard skip

Three days later tired bodies
Thousand euros lighter

We are surrounded by treated
Timber and concrete posts

Brother it's a new phase
Maintenance free gardening.

John O'Malley

LOCAL AREA
NETWORKS

I am connected
and you are connected,
there's more to friendship
than a shared IP
and the butt of a cigarette
passed between our lips
and I never loved you anyway,
I just failed to let you know.

My hands can bang
two keyboards at the same time,
I type at 122 words per minute
and still I use a notebook,
my dreams become memes,
my nightmares are novels,
I sleep easily when drunk
and not at all while sober,
I have fantastic, impractical ideas,
I lie about my age for no good reason
just because I can,
or maybe I'm lying about that,
'cause lies are the universal currency
and I am overdrawn.

Hack this,
DDoS my cut-throat
servers in Asia melting down,
air-conditioned
and full of illegal data,
you've got my inside measurement
and photographs of my penis,
probably
either low resolution
or shot with a zoom lens,
shot with an iPhone 5s,
shot with an air rifle
and a telescopic sight.

My brain is
wired.

Dane Cobain

TAKE OFF
FROM
LANDING

The brief co-habitation
Sits
Stuffed
Into Poundland laundry bags
On the landing
Homeward bound
To be picked over
Washed and aired
In Mother's
Sympathetic ear
Whilst Guy
She says
Stays on
Just a little
Singed
Around the edges
To see out
The tenure
And all the while
She's talking
I'm hoping
The doors close
A little more quietly
On their love
Than on their
Flat

Vennie

Fleet Street
Nelson, Lancashire, 1985

I first met Jane a month or two ago.
Not Zeno's Paradox but our too slow
And cautious courtship checked Time's arrow.

Somehow I cannot say the words I think.
She finds my coffee far too strong to drink,
So, while I play guitar, Jane slakes the sink.

She sings some folk songs, sitting on the floor.
Mine is not the conversation she'd been hoping for:
'What I mean is, if, so, because, well, either… or.'

Question and answer, it's almost like a grilling.
And then? Well, yes. Why not? We're both willing
And, after all, it's only time we're killing.

The trouble is, it simply won't stay dead;
Too briefly does the would-be quadruped
Possess the cosy cosmos of the bed.

We would possess the world but, lacking zeal,
Settle for a late Italian meal.
We start to say 'I know just how you feel…. '

How stealthily swim timid eyes;
Their deft evasive movements mesmerise.
Like everyone, we tell each other lies.

Graham Dawson

SHE DREAMS

She reclines,
and dreams
of being taken
by the hand
by a ballet dancer.

Standing proud,
he offers more,
a personal pas de deux.

She declines;
he pirouettes,
sashays away.

Virgo somnambulatio intacto.

Steve Allen

The Model

Through filmy white curtains
the sun blazed.
Fingers of light reached,
for the young woman
sitting silent, chin angled elegantly.

Utterly perfect, encased in youth
demure in her nudity.
Inside her head awareness
of their breathing, sighing – dropped charcoal,
muttered utterances heard through fog

Across the field outside
the racing shadowed form of a dog
thoughts of freedom, birds, trees.
Clock ticking, tension rising in
Bone
Blood
Muscle – body relaxes, dissolves, subsides.

Her day starts with a cycle ride
along a dual carriage way,
then country lanes slicked with leaves,
exhausting hills so steep she pushes.
A very, very long way

She arrives hot, always early
opens windows, doors
curtains fly in the breeze, she waits.
One day she said 'I feel unsteady, may I sit?'
then slides down the wall,

to sit slumped, a wilted flower,
they carried on drawing, painting
theirs a selfish love, not wanting
age or change to 'stretch' their skills
just beauty in a screaming world.

Yvonne Carter

TABULA RASA

At the heart of it all
were those fire sculptures,

the bowed bookshelves,
the standard lamp like the skeleton

of a long-legged bird
caught in the moment of blast,

but it was smoke that stole
into every fissure

of our lives, a storm creeping
from the horizon

of each white page,
blotting out butterflies and flowers,

smearing the walls,
sucked into cottons and silks,

nothing safe from it,
not even the wedding dress

I starved into, zippered
in its black body bag,

or that cascade
of sentimental muslin – smoke

that poured through the house
claiming books, beds, curtains, carpets, toys,

sweeping our past
like ballast out of a balloon,

until we were just so light
we lifted away.

Ruth Sharman

REVIEWS

Long Exposure at Cordoba **Katherine Crocker**
2012 Indigo Dreams Publishing,
ISBN: 978-1-907401-66-4   58pp   £6.99

How guilty I feel! Only now I sit down to this, though I've had the book – two copies, actually, one stolen by an erudite thief – for well over a year. Not like me. Doctoral thesis issues: writing, waiting, rewriting, re-waiting, and now even more waiting: too boring to go into. Plus other distractions; and my daughter moved 4000 miles. But at last, here we are.

This book, too, is about travel, and loss, moving on, and rediscovering joy; and recognizing our shared humanity. As an anthropologist, I'm already a softy for poems about non-western places, but the musicality and completeness of these word pictures only add to the attraction.

The title poem and cover art are a paean to her partner, their long relationship, and the ephemerality of ambition: the perfect shot – a 'long exposure' of multiple pillars – is marred by an image of the author. The immediacy of the moment is brought close by the photographer's sunburn ("midday pink").

Quite a few poems have previously appeared in notable journals: *The Rialto, Orbis, Acumen, Iota*; five are in anthologies. The most shocking is 'Istanbul, 1995', in which suicide is mere inconvenience, a "heap of old news". These poems – many are short, three or four stanzas long, less than 15 lines – are meant for the page, to be read, read again, with alternative meanings unlocked to lead the mind to different endings; much like tunes that whisper, tug the imagination to follow, long after notes have faded. Crocker is a singer, songwriter, musician and these skills are here.

Crocker rewrites myth and fairy-tale. In 'About Time', a twisted take on Cinderella tilts the story deliciously; in another, 'Daphne' becomes a tree. Slant rhymes move the poem:

> "......................In curls of cork
> he whispers love; too late his breath
> deadens in shells, once ears, now bark."

In 'Eurydice's story', the lovers fail again:

> "Simple,
> you would have thought. And so did I
> …Then he turned around. Why?"

The poem 'Daphne' is accompanied by a spare image – woodcut, one wants to say – that enhances, and even stands alone, as all illustrations should. Each of the few drawings that are scattered throughout similarly 'adds to' its poem, and is the work of Joseph Crocker.

The horror of massacres and displaced refugees haunt 'The Road', 'The Square' and 'Snake, Cheung Ek', and mingle with love, loss, and going on somehow ('Lovers, Belarus'; 'Wounded'; 'Lilacs'). Ageing too is treated with a kind, generous touch, in 'Lighthouse' and in 'Life lines':

> "All night, monitors flash primary colours,
> lines and numbers, maps of every moment
> she has."

Don't wait as long as I did to sit down with this book. Crocker writes that she is relatively new to poetry and in a way this is reflected in her fresh voice. Her musical background is evident in her attention to pacing and flow. Many poets on the festival scene and thus in the ear of a wide range of non-poetry buffs have either returned to using rhyme schemes or have rarely if ever altered their style. Crocker does not rhyme, but her poems have a wonderful rhythm which elevates them from vertical prose. We are invited with her as she travels, works, reminisces. 'Buttons' nudges out a memory of my own child's fascination, and how she too would do exactly this:

> "And the pleasure
> was not one single button
> but pushing my hands
> through the depth of them."

Rose Drew

Delicate Commemorations: *Missing Persons* **Patricia Averbach**
Ward Wood Publishing 2013
ISBN: 978-1-908742-23-0   pp 26   £3

Published as a result of winning the Lumen Camden Poetry Competition in 2013, this is Patricia Averbach's first poetry collection. A novelist as well as a poet, her poems often read like cut sections of narrative, sections of lives seen in close-focus. Family members, living and dead, beings both human and animal, take centre stage for a moment, are celebrated, then recede.

Averbach deals with loss in all its manifestations (of home and homeland, identity, vision and memory and well as family) and the continual adjustments each of these changes entails. She captures each 'disappearance' exactly – at times jolting the reader with the 'rightness' of a phrase – but she never manipulates our emotions by dwelling too long on a scene. This is economical poetry – as if the beings themselves don't want to overstay their welcome – indeed I would have liked more poems, and even greater depth.

Alongside unsentimental descriptions of disintegration we are shown Its antithesis – one that often emerges after a loss – a need to keep order. In 'Grandma's Ghost' her fastidious relative:

> "…turns to glare at me/annoyed that I've recalled/her hair standing up in crazy rows"
> and even gives advice:
> "The great chefs keep the kitchen clean."

In examining this need to keep life together, Averbach deftly turns to her Jewish heritage and the question (or not) of assimilation. In 'Survivors' we have a disappearance of another kind, that of cultural identity. By examining the gradual extinction of "gregarious" animals who were themselves shot, skinned and used as ornaments for those in power, she shows us the well-known actions of the World War II in a newly terrifying way. You make a bargain with Death, she suggests, either he takes you in fact, or in every way but fact. How far, she asks, do you sacrifice your individuality in order to survive?

The impossible demands of this 'double life' are examined again in the excellent 'Solomons's Baby at the Circus' in which the poet describes a daughter, given up for adoption, as divided, "strung between Jerusalem and Rome…a havdalah candle plunged in sacramental wine."

There is relief (although one can't call it light) in the midst of the intensity. There is a wry, behind-paw smile in 'Good Girl', in which the narrator (a dog) longs to reveal her true character:

> "We all thought I was safe.
> …
> So if I lay awake at night to watch
> the blood pulse thickly at your neck,
> there is no way you could have guessed.
> But the moon flashed one sharp tooth,
> bleeding light across the bed.
> Good girl, it said."

As in previous poems, a second, more truthful, self is kept secret.

Indeed Averbach finds humour in the most harrowing of circumstances. There is wry wit of 'The Book of Deborah,' in which the poet imagines her sister – who committed suicide in 2012 – as a goddess, designing a new, and wonderfully surreal, universe because "this one isn't working for her," and in 'Yartzheit,' when, as she remembers stories of her father's past, he returns to her:

"suddenly grown younger and stronger,
[turning] to ask if I remembered
the one about the rabbi and the elephant."

There is a daring ingenuity in "The Last Meals…", as well as a sense of the absurd. Ingenuity that this focus on food, which would usually stimulate the appetite, turns the stomach; absurdity in that a record should be kept. These are final requests for the modern age: voyeurism and bureaucracy together, in which the internet keeps a record of everything, forever.

However intense and personal these pieces; ultimately one is left with a sense of hope. Nowhere is this more evident than in the poem 'It Sometimes Happens.' However harrowing the situation, there is renewal, and delight must be taken, while we live. Anyone who has felt ground-shifting change of any kind will appreciate the gentle wisdom of her conclusion.

Tanya Nightingale

***The Final Take* Mario Susko**
Poetry Salzburg 2013
ISBN: 978 3 901993 39 8

'We have art in order not to perish of truth' wrote Nietzsche. In Mario Susko's work we have an art that portrays the process of perishing – it hangs at the edge and offers no consolation let alone the possibility of catharsis or redemption.

Susko remembers his mother,

'her book full of stories
that promised goodness and love
through suffering, the latter she
always took to be our undoing...'

The rope of the title, is, grotesquely, a child's skipping rope:

'We'll put you to sleep, they said,
unless we hear what we know you
know, a rope with orange handles
on the chair once a child's game.'

In finding a purchase on this work it is helpful, perhaps, to look at Shakespeare's tragedies. In 'Hamlet', Denmark passes into the hands of a prince whose heroic values are not worth an 'eggshell' and with a final, sickening twist, King Lear dies in the delusion that his daughter lives. These works are nihilistic rather than classically tragic and they defy the generations of critics who have attempted to make them so. Is there something in the zeitgeist of the Christian era that still hankers after redemption despite the merciless evidence of the 20th century with its industrialised wars and exterminations? Susko brings us face to face with our illusions.

The past is like a recurring cancer:

'I have overdosed on words, those that were
supposed to keep the past in remission.'

Searing images, associated with the war in Bosnia, emerge in poem after poem, in flashbacks symptomatic, perhaps, of post-traumatic stress. In 'The Final Take', the poem that gives the collection its title, they seem to be derived from a photograph. On the other hand, the photograph can also stand as a metaphor for compelling, indelible flashbacks:

'There is that tree, covered with plaster
and dust, left standing in the yard,
ghost-like, though somewhat defiant,
leaning toward the house reduced to rubble....'

As in all good poetry, the imagery does the talking, here reinforced by enjambment – 'plaster/and dust'. Susko's writing is sinuous, spare, meticulous, too urgent to be deflected by ornament. Often their contexts charge words and images with meaning until they resonate beyond the specific detail and evolve into symbolism:

'Lashing in and out, the waves
toy with pebbles around
my feet, making me go down
slowly into the shifting ground.'

Here we are presented with a moment of vertigo, powerfully tactile, where the body struggles for footing in the undermining surge.

'Someone comes to the end
of the lane and calls out,
Are you all right, and I respond,
I'm fine, thank you.
... I turn
around to watch him leave, his index
finger twirling at his temple.'

The persona is judged to be a madman. On the edge.

In 'A Theory of Knowing' Susko alludes to Yeats' 'The Second Coming'. Yeats wrote it in 1919 in the aftermath of the First World War – perhaps, also, he had the Irish Uprising of 1916 in mind:

'...Things fall apart; the centre cannot hold;
Mere anarchy is loosed upon the world,
The blood-dimmed tide is loosed, and everywhere
the ceremony of innocence is drowned....'

It's as if in the midst of the 'blood-dimmed tide' Susko remembers God's supposed omnipresence yet his immediate experience seems to provide no evidence of Divine presence. This allows Susko to develop a paradox: God,

'...kept us from knowing why something
can be everywhere by being nowhere –
and that was a cruel thing to do...'

It seems, on balance, 'The centre can probably hold...' (37) but in a context of profound metaphysical absence – that is, the state of absurdity.

One strategy for survival is to try to forget:

'I took pains to starve my memory,
practicing on as many things as I could,
some of them I lost intentionally:
my umbrella in a cab...
forcing myself to forget when and where –
I tried to remember phrases I'd used,
that got me where I am: life must go on,
things will turn out for the better...'

But the past is relentless:

'I'd stopped wearing a watch (They said he'd
been taken in at 10.30 pm and released
26 hours later, but no one has seen him
since/
...'

Susko allows himself no quarter – and neither does he allow it for the reader. This is a relentless read. There are, though, apparent gleams of light. Susko remembers with great fondness playing chess with his grandfather who maintains that in any game you play against two people – your antagonist but perhaps more importantly, yourself. After his grandfather's death he opens the box where the pieces are kept and begins to play, as it were, against his grandfather, 'the two of us playing furiously.' In the end, in great hilarity the game resolves to two lone kings – stalemate. The image is as resonant as any in the collection – this is a war game that cannot be resolved.

He inherits his grandmother's glasses and wears them in bed one night to see what might happen. The scene that plays out in his dreams involves the bewildering horrors of civil war;

> 'they barged in, now
> led by two of our next door neighbours
> grandma had sent food during the war,
> their rifle butts knocking down
> everything that was in their way.'

'Only a dream,' we say, to soothe a child's night terrors. But suppose that reality offers no solace, merely compounds the nightmare, that the domain of personal relationships offers no sure footing. The sands are shifting, undermining – poem after poem seems to lead to the brink of disintegration.

We have been here ourselves in the UK during the Wars of the Three Kingdoms, the civil, essentially religious wars, of the seventeenth century. And no doubt if they had had barbed wire and machine guns concentration camps would have proliferated. But our civil wars, perhaps the worst of all social catastrophes, are safely in the past, largely forgotten, soothed by the distance of centuries – except, of course, if you had happened to live in Northern Ireland during the Troubles.

Susko's poetry is hard on the emotions but perhaps should be required reading for anyone lulled by our comparative social stability. In the aftermath of the Jacobite rebellion of 1745/46, following the battle of Culloden, it is recorded that Government troops, near Inverness, roasted captive Jacobites, alive.

Henry Marsh

All Robert Powell
Valley Press 2015
ISBN: 9781908853448 96pp , £8.99

Rereading Robert Powell's new collection, *All,* I was struck again by the beautiful cover. Valley Press certainly make handsome books and this is no exception (though I did think at first they were coffee beans in that mug, not sunflower seeds!)

From the word go there is a feeling of confidence and strength about these poems but also a note of sadness. In the first poem 'The Poet Knocked', which is dedicated to Alan Jackson, it seems we are in the presence of a poet deciding whether to write:

> 'The poet knocked at my door
> as I sat dreaming at my desk

113

in that summer of hesitation
while the heron landed the dusk'

Although the poem is accessible in its language there is a mystery there
too. We are not told whether this is a ghostly or a living poet, the poet
does not answer the door and at the end tells us enigmatically 'only now
do I know what I knew'.

This theme of encountering the unknown continues so that, in 'Snapshot'
an image is thrown at the poet's feet

'a dark, thrown
present that gives you one more chance
to notice you're here and nowhere else'

In this first section of the book I particularly liked 'Light Passing Across
an Ancient City' which was inspired by the work of the artist, Jake
Attree. In it Powell does so much more than describe what is on the
canvas, though he does that beautifully too and the painting frees him to
see York in a new light. I like the way he broadens this out to include

'Ouse and Thames, Seine, Nile, Yangtze and Lethe,
with bridges for the boys of summer to leap from, laughing,
into the current of time.'

Another favourite among many was 'At a Yorkshire Wedding in
London', a personal poem just brimming with 'the thinginess of things',
people I can see and places I recognise:

'A small river, this one, where edge-water slips
like see-through muscle over the stones,
peat-dyed, ale-brown, down from the vast highways
of moors.'

'Owls in Dusk' stands out in the final section. I'm not at all surprised it
was a prize-winner. It is in a long tradition of poems in which the writer
encounters nature and is changed in some way. The power of the
creature, so beautifully caught

'your soft screams ripple out, old
into the pulsing tide
of car-hum, street voices, television'

leaves the poet vulnerable, self-questioning, honest:

'Holding a half-full cup I pause
to watch you in the chilled air
just beyond the lit floor
of the house, neck-deep
in a threadbare dressing gown
and October.'

114

as he asks

> 'So who is this boy, thrilled
> to see you tear quickly and go –'

Many of the poems are dedicated to friends and one thing which marks this collection as special for me is its examination and celebration of friendship, a subject so rarely written about and Powell does it so well. The reader feels in the company of a generous spirit and one who rejoices in company as well as in solitude. In 'The Hearing' it is the quiet company of a partner:

> 'Love, our hedge sparrows have flown with us on holiday:
> they flirt with the locals in the olives by Lake Garda'

and he writes about her and about poetry while she sleeps on the balcony.

In 'Winter Text' he's 'Dutiful Dad' delivering paraphernalia to help his son make snowmen in a graveyard and there's real affection and regret in 'childhood's last night'.

For these are peopled poems, friends and relations dart in and out of them, are addressed, remembered, valued. A fellow poet lends his copy of Charles Simic 'he no doubt thought I needed some help' but ends up with the poet's gratitude for what he finds and writes about inside its pages.

There is a real love of books and of writing often expressed here, and a love too of the act of writing, of opening yourself to what is around you to enable that to happen:

> 'This gives permission for the morning, the breeze, and
> certain shadows to rub against your leg, mindful and
> reassuring, with their strange remembered fur.'
>
> (from 'Open')

An apprentice poet could learn a great deal from Powell's calm, open mindfulness, from his facility with language and his deep respect for books as well as from his confident way of writing about, or at least starting from, everyday contact with loved ones or startling encounters with the wild.

I enjoyed every minute of reading and rereading Robert Powell's poems and I like to think of him as 'The Missing Child' wandering off to answer the call of writing:

> 'And they are still looking for me,
> but I was no longer there.
> I was here,
> writing this.'

Carole Bromley

Clarity in Distance? *Zig Zag* **Martin Bates**
pub: White Adder Press 2014
ISBN 978-0-9520827-5-0   pp. 87   £8.50

You can recognise a new collection from an inexperienced writer from a mile away: brimming with energy, but with a tendency to want to deal with every subject under the sun, a 'give 'em everything you've got' attitude to formal verse and a wish to change the world. Martin Bates' new book, 'Zig Zag' is far from this. He does indeed present us with the world (taking us to Wales, Spain, India, Egypt and Tibet) but with the control, detachment and reserve of a mature poet.

His visual acuity and ability to convey those sights is redolent of the Welsh poets Edward Thomas and R S Thomas. His vivid descriptions of foreign sights notwithstanding however, to my mind he is at his most persuasive when describing the rural scenes of the British Isles: 'April', (written at Ty Newydd) 'The gardener' and 'A fawn one afternoon' being examples. For Bates, the growth of the natural world and the growth of writing itself cannot be separated: each is essential to the other.

The first section (headed 'Alone under the moon') illustrates his overall title perfectly: poems do indeed zig-zag from home to abroad, from the exotic to the domestic and back again. It is in this opening section, I feel, that we see some of Bates' most emotionally engaged poems, as in 'Old Boy' and 'The kitchen', in which he is aware of his own emotional confusion:

> Your sudden tears like summer rain
> flummox me.
> What did I say? What did I do?
> Ham-fisted, I argue. You don't reply.
> What did I say?
> …
> Where did they come from
> these tears?"   ('The kitchen.')

Engaging and beautiful as his descriptions are, I would have liked more response to those descriptions. In his poem 'I see the mountain' for example (in a section dealing with his travels though India and the Himalayas), he writes:

> "Leviathan looming
> from sees of sleep
> musing jade and malachite…
>
> Under the mountain I wait
> restless as an ant
> freeing its feelers from dust.

…
I see the mountain. I feel
the mountain sees me."

What is he waiting for? Why is he restless? He feels the mountain's eye
upon him – does he feel it still as he continues through the rest of his
journey? I wanted him to take us as far into his internal life as into his
geographical one.

Indeed through all his travels I feel he shows us frustratingly little of his
own attitudes and reflections. Even in what is possibly his most personal
poem, an elegy for his mother, we are kept at a distance:

"I stole to your ear
whispered the words
I could not say out loud.
Once as a child
when we walked hand-in-hand
I was playing with the words…
'I like you very much'
came out instead"   (A Florin')

He is a writer of an earlier era, part of a generation in which intimate
feelings were not spoken of and private matters were kept private. Today
we are used to seeing emotions expressed on social media every day,
perhaps to our detriment. However one function of poetry is to allow us
access to our emotions, to express the very personal, and that to engage it
must do just that. Even though I can guess what those words were, I
would have liked to have been told.

Having said that, he has an undeniable ability to convey the visual world.
Much as we may long to know more of his inner life, there is no denying
the potency of the scenes he paints, as in the two 'month' poems: the
previously mentioned 'April' and 'Riding home in August'- one long
unfolding sentence in which every word is both necessary and perfectly
placed.

Bates' careful reserve serves the poetry best in section six, 'The past is
another country,' addressing (in the main) his memories of the Second
World War – a time of murmured rumour, misunderstood presences
(barrage balloons that seemed "so pretty") when nothing was fully
explained. In such a climate, memories, so necessary for poetry, are seen
as "naughty" and "saboteurs" derailing official instructions or vital but
mundane trains of thought. This was a time when, for the sake of
survival, feelings and opinions had to be kept under wraps. Tellingly, it
is this lack of expression that is expressed most effectively and provides
the heart of the collection.

Mention should be made of the sketches preceding each section of the book by his son, the artist Alexander Bates. Each referring in some way to the section they illustrate, they are dense enough to remind one of etchings, adding to the aesthetic quality of the book as a whole. This collection has the sense of summation; of someone gathering together all the disparate people and places he has encountered. Let's hope there is much more to come.

Tanya Nightingale

On Light and Carbon **Noel Duffy**
Ward Wood Publishing 2013,
ISBN: 978-1-908742-04-9 pp71 £8.99

It is rare for me to feel I can't put a poetry collection down. Usually I dip in and savour. *On Light and Carbon* held me from the opening lines of the first poem. 'Earthrise' is based on the words of earth Gene Cernan, Commander of Apollo 17.

> I saw it
> all blue and swirling cloud
> before   me,
> small as a marble.
> I could have almost reached out
> and retrieved it
> from the blackness…

It captures beautifully the wonder of seeing earth from space and sets the tone of the whole collection. Duffy never talks down to his reader, but he does not flinch from introducing material that is not usually considered 'poetic'. The themes of his collection are wide-ranging. Poems about family and friends, ageing and childhood, sit easily beside meditations on the excitement of scientific discovery, past and present. Titles like 'CM142: Classical Mechanics', 'Harmonic Resonance' and 'Microscope' are rare in poetry collections, but here feel perfectly in place, alongside 'Trinity Ball' or 'Old Shoes', 'God of Small Things' or 'Keepsake'.

The personal poems, like 'Last Days', 'Photograph' and the sequence 'Timepieces', appear conversational – even simply written – but their craftsmanship is impressive. Duffy catches the moment in a few brief lines, carefully controlled emotion conveyed through apparently mundane situations. His precise language and accurate observations linger in the memory.

> I don't know why I did it,
> sneaking out of the house

after dinner, and crawling into
the gap between the wall
and the garage. I watched
the wood-lice at my feet
make small patterns in the dirt… ('Hide and Seek')

For me, however, the poems that blend scientific fact with poetic vision are even more memorable. Duffy has the rare ability to convey challenging ideas in a very readable form. He brings figures from the history of science and astronomy to life, catching their tone and period in apparently effortless verse. Only the notes at the back reveal how much research lies behind the conversational tone.

In 'On Light', for example, Duffy tells the story of Ibn al-Haytham, known as Alhazen, punished for failing to keep his promise to regulate the flood waters of the Nile. His observations from his prison window laid the foundations of our knowledge of the properties of light. Yet when released from gaol Alhazen's response is quietly dignified, anticipation of the ordinary pleasures of life replacing anger.

So he sits in his chair looking at this window
for the final time, nostalgic for all it has
given him. He stands at last and turns to door
He thinks he might like to go to the market
and buy fresh pomegranates.

Any poet who can also explain the second law of thermodynamics in a few concise lines deserves admiration.

The law is simple and profound:
the hot cools down.
Take for example this cup of tea that I hold.
Forgetting it for a time while
I spoke on the phone, I return
to find it already cold, the heat
drained from it into this small room. ('The 2nd Law')

Occasionally the language is a little too predictable, or the style too conversational for me, as in 'Night Watch' and 'The Older Artist'. Such poems feel a little flat compared to others in the collection. They are in the minority, and still interesting to read. I loved this book.

Pauline Kirk

A Voyage to Babylon **Henry Marsh**
Maclean Dubois 2013
ISBN: 978095627844 106pp £10

The centrepiece of Henry Marsh's fifth full-length collection is a vast
poetic sequence charting the fate of a group of Scots Covenanters,
imprisoned and exiled in the 17th century for defying the English Crown
and the Episcopalian church. The sequence interweaves narrative, diary,
internal monologue and nature poetry to considerable dramatic effect,
allowing the reader a privileged insight into a dark and often overlooked
chapter in British history.

A Voyage to Babylon is no mere period piece, though. The 21st century,
like the 17th, is a landscape where religious fundamentalists, liberal
humanists and atheist militants all too easily become pawns in the power
games of political vested interests. When Marsh writes about the
experience of the prisoners transported on the *Henry and Francis*, he is
well aware that there are communities experiencing equivalent injustices
today.

John Fraser, the central character in the drama, was a real person, who
survived exile to return to Scotland as a rural Presbyterian minister.
Through his eyes we follow the Covenanters from arrest and internment,
via a brutal transportation across the Atlantic, to a new life in a fledgling
America.

This is a *tour de force* of character-driven poetry. Fraser is a devout
Christian, but never a fundamentalist. He knows that

> "the spirits
> that vaunt [God's] authority are the same
> that destroy in its name... Their God becomes infernal."

His questioning of, and struggling with, his God provides an impassioned
counterpoint to the bleak narratives of death, disease and poverty which
were the lived experience of the transported Covenanters. Here is a man
who knows the bloody consequences of religious extremism, "the
glittering eye, that pounding certitude". He chooses to be a peacemaker –
"mercifully wordless, / a kindly presence" – in spite of the personal and
political difficulties which come with that choice. He becomes an agent
of reconciliation in his own community and amongst the Native
American peoples; and when he finally returns to Scotland to live out his
last years; he can look upon his homeland with unclouded eyes.

It is rare to find contemporary British poetry which portrays Christian
faith in such a sympathetic light. The language of "soul" is nowadays too
quickly dismissed as "curious and archaic" (as the adjudicator of one
recent poetry competition put it). The strength of Marsh's writing is that

John Fraser is a wholly believable man of soul: a "knot of contradiction", but a wise, generous hearted individual whose humanity (in the warmest sense of the word) sings from every poem.

The supporting cast of characters are no less sympathetic: his beloved Jean, whose earthy, no-nonsense compassion provides the anchor for Fraser's frequent storms of self-doubt; hot-headed James Forsyth, whose wife and newborn son perish on the journey to the New World; Lady Athunie, forced to renounce her high birth to join the exiles on the *Henry and Francis*, but who never sees her destination. A voice of doubt accompanies them: a rationalist philosopher who's questioning of the fundamentalists' blind acceptance of their fate provides an essential counterpoint to Fraser's crises of faith and Forsyth's grief and disillusionment. The names are those of real people from the passenger manifest of the ship; but apart from the records of their deaths, the rest is Marsh's own invention.

The collection begins with a foreword from Marsh's colleague Alexander McCall Smith. Whilst I can't disagree with the good professor about Marsh's considerable talent as a storyteller, I don't entirely concur with his effusive praise for the poet's writing style. The character poems are compelling, and there is some beautiful nature writing to counterpoint the sad tales of the passengers on the *Henry and Francis*. But there are also a great many 'poems' which are really pieces of narrative divided into lines and stanzas to mimic a verse structure, and which in my mind would have been better presented as short prose sections rather than as a semblance of poetry. These are short on imagery, largely lacking in any poetic musicality, and over-stuffed with unnecessary small words ('the's, adjectives, adverbs such as "seemingly"). This book would not have been any less a poetry collection had the narrative sections been laid out as prose. Presenting them as poetry lends the sequence an air of repetitiveness which does not do justice to the splendid writing in the truly poetic pieces.

The collection also includes two shorter sections, predominantly of nature poetry, set firmly in the 21st century. The *Scribbles* are mainly dedicated to friends and family. Apart from *March 17th*, a delightfully idiosyncratic poem centred around a frog stranded on a pavement, I felt rather distant from the scenes and the people at the heart of these poems and I didn't really bond with them. There was a uniformity of style and voice about these poems, and I found myself longing for a change in the weather.

This was supplied in the final sequence, *West and East*, a beautiful series of meditations on the ever varying moods of the seas and skies surrounding Scotland, which separate the poet from many of those he loves. "This is the sea where night gathers," he declares in the opening of

North Sea. Marsh is at his most honest, most vulnerable when surrounded by waves and open sky. "I think the North Sea is my father," he confesses in *At St Cyrus*. He may well be right.

This is not a flawless collection. I looked for a little more variation of voice, some truly original imagery, and I wasn't wholly satisfied. What I *did* find was exquisite natural-world poetry, a gripping journey into Scottish history, and a moving contemplation of what it means to be a fully alive human and a person of faith. These poems

> "sing / of the faith that things
> can speak for us – wind and sea,
> the golden moon and the light
> that is passing to darkness."

And that, ultimately, is what I look to all poetry to do.

Andy Humphrey

Other anthologies and collections available from Stairwell Books

First Tuesday in Wilton	Ed. Rose Drew and Alan Gillott
The Exhibitionists	Ed. Rose Drew and Alan Gillott
The Green Man Awakes	Ed. Rose Drew
Fosdyke and Me and Other Poems	John Gilham
frisson	Ed. Alan Gillott
Gringo on the Chickenbus	Tim Ellis
Running With Butterflies	John Walford
Late Flowering	Michael Hildred
Scenes from the Seedy Underbelly of Suburbia	Jackie Simmons
Pressed by Unseen Feet	Ed. Rose Drew and Alan Gillott
York in Poetry Artwork and Photographs	Ed. John Coopey and Sally Guthrie
Rosie and John's Magical Adventure	The Children of Ryedale District Primary Schools
Her House	Donna Marie Merritt
Taking the Long Way Home	Steve Nash
Chocolate Factory	Ed. Juliana Mensah and Rose Drew
Skydive	Andrew Brown
Still Life With Wine and Cheese	Ed. Rose Drew and Alan Gillott
Somewhere Else	Don Walls
Sometimes I Fly	Tim Goldthorpe
49	Paul Lingaard
Homeless	Ed. Ross Raisin
Satires	Andy Humphrey
The Ordinariness of Parrots	Amina Alyal
New Crops from Old Fields	Ed. Oz Hardwick
Throwing Mother in the Skip	William Thirsk-Gaskill

For further information please contact rose@stairwellbooks.com

www.stairwellbooks.co.uk
@stairwellbooks